COMPTOIR
LIBANAIS *express*

COMPTOIR
LIBANAIS *express*

preface

Comptoir Libanais Express is about the way I like to eat and about flavours and combinations that just taste right. Deep down I'll always be a rebel in my approach to food. I like to bring together a huge mezze of ideas based on what I want to eat at that moment then share it with generosity and ease. I'm as likely to eat fried chicken in Beirut as ful medamas in London. Be brave, try different things, and just go where your hunger takes you.

Tony Kitous

Contents

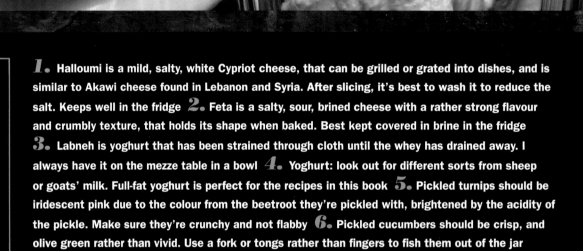

ingredients

1. Halloumi is a mild, salty, white Cypriot cheese, that can be grilled or grated into dishes, and is similar to Akawi cheese found in Lebanon and Syria. After slicing, it's best to wash it to reduce the salt. Keeps well in the fridge **2.** Feta is a salty, sour, brined cheese with a rather strong flavour and crumbly texture, that holds its shape when baked. Best kept covered in brine in the fridge **3.** Labneh is yoghurt that has been strained through cloth until the whey has drained away. I always have it on the mezze table in a bowl **4.** Yoghurt: look out for different sorts from sheep or goats' milk. Full-fat yoghurt is perfect for the recipes in this book **5.** Pickled turnips should be iridescent pink due to the colour from the beetroot they're pickled with, brightened by the acidity of the pickle. Make sure they're crunchy and not flabby **6.** Pickled cucumbers should be crisp, and olive green rather than vivid. Use a fork or tongs rather than fingers to fish them out of the jar

7. Carob, mulberry or pomegranate molasses, has a rich, sour flavour and makes a great dressing
8. Nuts in the shell might seem old-fashioned but the whole business of shelling them after dinner has a sweet charm for me. Bring them back into fashion **9.** You won't see pickled green almonds often but in the Lebanon they're a treat. They're crisp, refreshing and perfect served with cocktails or a mezze **10.** When you're buying fresh pomegranate, go for the heaviest ones that are firm all over, without bruising **11.** Melon, ice-cold and cut fresh, is perfect served after a meal. One of the simplest and best desserts I know **12.** Quince is one of the most revered fruits. Either bake them whole or peel, core and simmer barely covered in water until soft **13.** Keep a stack of flatbreads well-wrapped in the freezer as they warm in minutes in a hot oven. Essential for every mezze table.

Comptoir
glossary & basics

Allspice

Allspice is one of the principal spices used in Lebanese cuisine. It is the dried fruit of the Pimenta Dioica tree and is believed to have been called allspice by the British, who thought it combined the flavours of cinnamon, cloves and nutmeg. It lends a warmth and earthy flavour to Lebanese food and is subtly able to lift dishes that might initially appear quite bland.

Apple Vinegar

You can use cider vinegar in place of Lebanese apple vinegar, though the flavour is not as complex. Traditionally we make it each autumn by simply chopping the apples without peeling or coring, then we place them in a barrel and leave them somewhere warm for a few months until the fermentation has slowed and the liquid has a rich vinegar aroma. Lebanese apple vinegar has a dark golden colour and is slightly cloudy, as it's unfiltered and retains more of the apple. We use it often in marinades, as it's very good with grilled meats, or sometimes on a salad I'll use it in place of lemon juice. If you have the time, you can intensify the flavour of shop-bought cider vinegar by grating 1–2 raw apples into a bowl containing 500ml cider vinegar, covering it with a cloth, and leaving it at room temperature for a week before straining and rebottling. This will give the cider vinegar much more flavour.

Aubergines

Perhaps the most important vegetable we use at Comptoir, and in Lebanese cooking. When it's cooked its texture is porous enough to hold the oils, spices and sauces you mix it with, while adding a flavour that softens rather than dominates the dish. The most famous recipe is perhaps baba ghanoush, made by roasting eggplants, peeling the skin off, mixing the finely chopped flesh with tahini until thick, then adjusting the flavour to taste with lemon juice, mashed raw garlic, chopped parsley and salt. See page 56 for my twist on the classic version – my 'red' baba ghanoush.

Baharat spice

A Middle Eastern spice mix that varies according to the country and to the cook – each has their own and many argue endlessly over the precise balance of spices. In Morocco rosebuds are added to the mix…

You can buy Baharat at some specialist supermarkets in the UK, but it's easy to mix it yourself at home too: 1½ teaspoons of paprika with 1 teaspoon each of ground black pepper and cumin, ¾ teaspoon each of ground coriander, cinnamon, clove and nutmeg, and ¼ teaspoon of ground cardamom. Store in a jar and use within 3 months. Baharat spice is excellent mixed with yoghurt and used as a simple marinade on meat before grilling or baking. You can also combine mixed spice with paprika, cumin and black pepper for a similar flavour.

Basturma

The most popular cured meat in Lebanon is this cured beef, similar to the Italian bresaola or the American pastrami, though with a much stronger, more distinctive spiced flavour. It's made by salting the meat, then squeezing out any liquid before rubbing it with a paste of spices. Basturma has a deep rich flavour that suits soft, mild-flavoured cheeses and pickles so will most commonly be served as part of a mezze spread.

Basturma is quite hard to find in the UK and although you can substitute it with bresaola or pastrami, you could also make something more akin to it yourself by sprinkling slices of cooked beef with a mixture of ground cumin, fenugreek, chilli powder and paprika, and leaving them to sit for 1 hour in the fridge before serving.

Bread

No Lebanese cook would consider serving their meal without some type of bread. Bread is the backbone of our cuisine. So, whether it be pitta bread as a vehicle for scooping up copious amounts of dips or sauces; saj bread as a vessel for soaking up the juices of a pile of shawarma or koftas, warm cheese and lamb-topped man'ousha, or simply served warm from the oven spread with a simple topping of za'atar mixed with olive oil for breakfast, bread will be on the table at every time of the day.

The problem is that the word 'flatbread', which is what most Middle Eastern breads are, makes it sound as though they would be simple to make. Not at all. Indeed, if ever you get the opportunity to watch these breads being made – seize it. The skill required to make the paper-thin expanses of dough is extraordinary, and watching the baker fling the bread in the air to stretch and massage it without breaking it is incredible.

Saj, another type of flatbread cooked on a domed griddle over which the dough is stretched and baked, is equally technical and requires years of practice to perfect the technique.

And while even in the Middle East, making bread isn't something cooks do at home – the bakers' versions are just too good to pass up – it is possible to have a go yourself. Following Dan's simple recipe below, you can create something that's similar to the breads we enjoy in Lebanon – not as thin necessarily, but hugely tasty, and a fun thing at which to try your hand.

Flatbread dough

To make a simple flatbread, dissolve 1 teaspoon fast-action yeast and 1 tablespoon sugar in 400ml warm water, add 2 tablespoons olive oil then 600g strong white bread flour and 1 teaspoon salt. Mix everything together well, knead lightly then cover and leave to rise for an hour before using.

Sometimes I'll just divide it into about 10 balls, roll them thinly and just bake them on a griddle in batches. Alternatively, if you want some puffed-up pittas, get the oven very hot (around 240°C/220°C fan/gas 9), roll the dough pieces about 5mm thick and bake on a baking sheet until they puff up – about 4–6 minutes.

Broad beans

In Arab countries we call these beans ful (pronounced 'fool') and they're simply dried broad beans. There's a famous Egyptian dish that you find everywhere in the region, even in tins, called ful medamas or pot-cooked beans, that are served very soft and mixed with oil or butter, tomato, spices and seasoning. It's a popular breakfast dish, which might sound strange, but is it really any different to opening a tin of baked beans? Served with some warm pitta it makes a nourishing and warming start to the day. When dry the beans look a rather unappetising shade of brown, but cooked they have the most rich and complex flavour. Often they're used soaked and ground to a rough paste with chickpeas to make falafel, as they have a starchier texture and hold the falafel together better.

Bulgar wheat

This grain, what we call burghul (pronounced 'burgle'), is made from durum wheat that has been cooked, dried and cracked. It's a village food and when I get invited to people's homes I've tasted it cooked different ways. In the old days the husked wheat grains would be washed by the edges of the river and left to dry in the sun on woven mats, the same ones we'd place under trees to collect the olives or dry grapes on. Then it would be boiled until the grain doubled in size, drained and left to dry again in the hot sun. Finally the bulgar would be placed in sacks and carted to the local mill where most would be ground either fine or coarse, with the remainder milled into bulgar flour. Being pre-cooked and dried means it is very quick to prepare, like couscous. Fine bulgar is used for kibbeh, while the coarse type is good for pilaf or salads.

Carob

In the West we sometimes think of carob as a chocolate substitute, but in Lebanon it has a much more traditional place. Carob trees are almost as common as olive trees there, and so the use of the seeds from the tree as a flavouring is more typical. You can often find carob powder in health food shops, and it is true that you can use cocoa as a substitute. Harder to find is carob molasses, which is extracted from the coarsely ground seeds that are then soaked and simmered to release the flavour. The strained liquid is then reduced and has a naturally sweet flavour and syrupy consistency.

Cheese (see also Labneh)

There are three main types of cheese used in the recipes in this book – halloumi, feta and labneh (for more on labneh, see 20). These choices do reflect authenticity – all three are commonly used throughout the Middle East – but they've also been deliberately chosen to account for what it's possible to source here in the UK. The Middle East does not have a strong association with cheese-making. The climate and the quality of the soil has meant that the animals' diet doesn't have the same rich flavours of that of their European cousins so the basic flavour of the cheese is often quite bland, something that tends to be countered by upping the salt content.

Halloumi is a Cypriot cheese that has become popular across the Middle East, particularly in Turkey and the Levant. If you've not tried it, personally I think you're in for a treat, though I admit that its unusual characteristics do divide opinion. Halloumi is very salty and has quite a rubbery texture. It is traditionally made from a mixture of goat and sheep's milk and is most commonly served grilled or fried to caramelise the squeaky exterior and up the flavour, but you can also serve it plain – try my marinated version on page 174. Although you might think that the salt would be too dominating, halloumi works well in many different contexts. Its most common herb partner is mint, while it's as happy being served in a tomato salad as it is alongside sweet figs.

Feta is a crumbly tangy curd cheese made either purely from sheep's milk or from a mixture of sheep and goat's milk. EU legislation now dictates that only cheeses made in the traditional way within mainland Greece and certain Greek islands may be called 'feta', although variations on the brined salty cheese are made across the Eastern Mediterranean basin, often known simply as 'white cheese'. Feta is wonderfully versatile – toss it through salads, blend it with thick yoghurt, lemon and seasoning to make a dip, or even serve it in sweet contexts, with honey and figs, as a hybrid cheese–dessert course.

Chickpeas

The essential ingredient for hummus, since the word hummus means 'chickpeas' in Arabic. As they're one of the oldest cultivated pulses they have been always a staple on the Arabic table. In Lebanon, chickpeas are mainly grown in the Beqaa Valley, and at markets in Beirut (only 30km from the valley) you can find different varieties that have been hand-picked and sun dried. Don't buy too many at a time, as their flavour changes the longer they sit in the cupboard.

Chilli

One of the great misconceptions the West has with Arabic food in general is the expectation that all the flavours will be fiery. Except for a few dishes like muhammara, you won't find many chillies in our food, although it's

ingredients

1. For the best flavour buy shelled walnuts in small quantities **2.** Pine nuts are best toasted on a tray in the oven, as they cook unevenly in a frying pan **3.** To get that really vivid green from pistachios, cover them with boiling water for 10–15 minutes till the skins can be slipped off with your fingers **4.** Fine bulgar wheat is made from cooked, dried and cracked wheat grains, needs very little soaking before use and is great for fattoush salad **5.** Wholewheat brown bulgar is made from the whole grain, has dark colour and is best for cooked dishes **6.** Coarse bulgar can be used like fine but needs a longer soaking time **7.** Freekeh is young green wheat that has been roasted and cracked **8.** Long-grain rice is best for the recipes in this book. Go for the best quality, with few broken grains **9.** Toasted vermicelli is excellent stirred into pilaf. Buy it ready-toasted or fry the dry pasta in oil until golden before boiling it. **10.** Za'atar is essentially dried ground herbs, mixed with sesame and spices, and sometimes roasted flour so it's not always gluten-free

11. Cinnamon sticks can be removed from cooking when the flavour is spiced enough **12.** Sumac is a dried, ground berry, that adds a bright tart flavour **13.** For me, cardamom is an essential store-cupboard spice **14.** Allspice is actually one spice, with a fragrant mild flavour, best freshly ground **15.** Split dried and peeled broad beans are excellent mixed in equal part with chickpeas in falafel, as they help it hold together better **16.** Whole dried broad beans are typically soaked and slow-cooked, and have the richest flavour of any bean I know **17.** Whole red lentils have a different character to the split kind, as they hold their shape well in cooking **18.** Dried mulukhiyah is a type of mallow, and is almost a store cupboard green vegetable. Soak it then cook it lightly, it's excellent flavoured with lemon in soup **19.** Chickpeas are the most essential bean in the Lebanese kitchen, and a must-have in the cupboard. Look for the tiny ones, they're the most prized for their delicate flavour.

true that a small amount is often used. When we want to add chillies, the easiest way is by adding a paste. In Lebanon, chilli paste is used as a way of adding heat but typically in a very subtle way. You can make it at home very easily. Traditionally we'd just make a paste of the raw chillies, spread it out, and let it dry in the sun, but you can achieve something similar, even in a cooler climate. Choose long red chillies (the hotness of the final paste will depend on their fieriness), trim and discard the ends, then roast them gently at about 120°C/100°C fan/gas ¼ for 2 hours. Then discard the seeds and purée the flesh finely in a food processor with a little salt and olive oil. If you'd prefer to buy it, then look for harissa, a north African chilli paste, similar to the Lebanese sort but with the addition of garlic, spices and occasionally tomato paste.

Coffee

Though Italian-style coffee is as popular in Beirut as any other fashionable city, there is another older way to prepare coffee that we call Ahweh Arabi, and it's usually drunk in the morning. Take a teaspoon of finely ground coffee and a coffee cup of water (per person) and heat this in a small saucepan with a pinch of ground cardamom and – if you like it sweet – a teaspoon of sugar. Bring the coffee to the boil then remove from the heat, let it cool slightly then let it boil and rest again. Repeat this one more time then add sugar to taste and serve black and piping hot. You are left with a thick, strong liquid. Whenever I'm using coffee in sweet dishes, like cakes and ice creams, I like to add a little ground cardamom as a nod to this older method.

Cumin

A flick through the ingredients lists in the book show you what a fundamental spice cumin is in Lebanese cuisine and indeed in most parts of the Arab world. You either use the seeds, which should be toasted to bring out their nutty, peppery aroma, or the ground spice, which is more commonly used alongside other spices in blends or to flavour soups and stews.

Figs

Fig trees are to Lebanon what apple trees are to the UK – we're lucky to have an abundance. In fact so widespread are fig trees that many households end up with a glut of the fruit and need to preserve them. Thick, sticky fig jam is therefore another staple on our table, spread on flatbreads at breakfast time or served as a sweet accompaniment to cheese. It's really easy to make your own and will keep for up to a month in the fridge after opening. Take 200g green figs – slightly green ones are best as they are on the point of ripening and will have the strongest flavour. Roughly chop, discarding the tops, and place in a pan with the juice of 1 lemon. Simmer for about 5 minutes then add 200g granulated sugar and stir to dissolve, then bring to the boil and simmer gently for about 5 minutes or until you have a jammy consistency. Leave a little liquid in the mixture as the jam will thicken as it cools. Transfer to sterilised jars and store in a cool, dark place until ready to use. Use generously!

Garlic

Though from the outside Lebanese food is sometimes thought of as being a cuisine intensely flavoured with garlic, that's actually not true. Garlic is used sparingly in Lebanon, and though they do use intense garlic sauces it's not a staple in all savoury recipes as it has increasingly become in the West. I tend to either accompany a dish with a garlic sauce if I want my guests to have the flavour intense, otherwise I use it discreetly so the flavour enhances rather than overpowers the dish.

Honey

Choose well-flavoured honey for the best flavour in Lebanese cooking. I found one of my favourite honeys at the Souk el Tayeb in Beirut, run by my friend Kamal Mouzawak. There they have honey from bees that collect the nectar from cedar and oak trees, and the resulting honey has an opaque terracotta appearance and a curious caramel flavour.

Labneh

Labneh is found across the Middle East. It is yoghurt that has had most of its liquid strained until it is almost as thick as cream cheese (how thick it becomes will depend on how long you strain it and how you like it). Where on a British table you might have a jar of mayonnaise, in Lebanon you'll find labneh serving almost the same role – as a dip, a cool accompaniment to grilled meats or fish, or as part of a mezze spread where it would be served on a plate, drizzled with oil and scattered with the host's choice of seasoning – fresh herbs, za'atar, chopped olives, even some chopped vegetables.

Throughout the book I've suggested using labneh in sauces or dips and as an accompaniment, so it's worth having a go at making your own so that you've always got a batch to hand. The great thing about it is that once it's made it can be kept for up to a week.

Take a medium sieve or colander big enough to hold 500g of thick yoghurt. Sit the sieve over a bowl. Wet then wring out a muslin cloth or tea towel so that it's damp, and press it inside the mesh of the sieve. Some cooks like to salt the labneh at this point – I don't – but if you like, just stir a little salt in with the yoghurt to taste, remembering that it will intensify in flavour as it drains. Pour the yoghurt into the cloth and then leave it undisturbed in the fridge overnight. At first you might think that it's draining so slowly that nothing is happening but have faith. Overnight the liquid will drip away and leave a thick yoghurt that's much smoother and cheese-like. Serve it right away or store in the fridge, covered.

Mezze

Eating food at Comptoir, as in Lebanon, is all about sharing, and the way we do that is by having lots of small dishes on the table at once so that everyone can try a spoonful from different dishes as opposed to separate plates served to each guest. We call this way of eating a mezze (pronounced mez-ay), and it's our tradition rather than a modern thing. With the recipes in the book, think about having a few different dishes on the table for the meal, some served cold and made ahead combined with other quickly prepared recipes.

Mint

What I miss most about Beirut is the huge bunches of mint you see at the markets. You sometimes find them at Asian shops here, but there's something slightly depressing about the tiny packets containing just a few sprigs that you usually see at the supermarkets. In our kitchen we have so many uses for mint: infused to make a type of tea, chopped and mixed with labneh or yoghurt, steeped in syrup to make a cold drink or sorbet, chopped into salads or mixed with raw meat. What I'm really saying is make the most of it and don't waste it. Put fresh mint in a man'ousha or a wrap and it changes the whole flavour. It can even be dried in a low oven so that the leaves can be crumbled. It loses that fresh aroma but instead takes on a curious flavour closer to black tea that we use in some dishes. When you buy mint, don't be in a rush to wash it and don't just cram it into a corner of the fridge like a cabbage. Treat it with the care you'd give to fresh flowers: have a jug ready filled with water, trim the ends off the mint and quickly immerse the stalks in the jug. This way the mint will keep fresh for days at room temperature.

Nuts

Used generously in all parts of our cooking, sometimes in surprising ways. Chopped or whole nuts add crunch and texture, ground nuts thicken and bulk, and let's not even get into the myriad flavours – salty and sweet – that nuts provide. Nuts will often be the crowning glory in a dish, scattered over at the end to complete and contrast.

Pistachios and pine nuts are particular favourites of mine but you're likely to be cooking with all sorts. Experiment – swap my choices for your own and see what works for you.

Nuts can go rancid if not stored properly so it's best to store them in airtight containers. Buy them in small batches and replace regularly – I wouldn't keep them for any longer than a month as they can go soft.

Orange blossom water

Made by distilling the blossom of sour orange trees, it lends a delicate flavour to pastries, syrups and drinks but needs to be used sparingly as the strength of the liquid can be pretty strong and it can easily overpower. Use less than you need to begin with; you can always add more.

Pickles

Essential for every mezze table. The most curious are those electric pink turnip pickles, made by curing raw turnips with a slice of raw beetroot. More common are cucumber pickles made traditionally by leaving cucumbers to ferment in slightly acidic water so the bacteria on the skins sours the flavour. To keep them crisp vine leaves are often added to the pickle. If you have leftover pickled cucumbers they make an excellent pickle sauce, great spooned over hummous or a butterbean dip (page 192). To make it roughly chop 1 large gherkin and put with a handful of chopped fresh dill or parsley in a food processor. Whizz it together while slowly adding enough olive oil to make a smooth paste then salt to taste, then refrigerate.

Pomegranate

Pomegranates are native to Iran but they are used extensively throughout the Middle East in many different forms – seeds, juice, or once boiled and reduced, as pomegranate molasses (syrup) – they are one of the most versatile fruits I can think of.

Extracting the seeds from the whole fruit looks complicated but is actually very simple. Cut the pomegranate in half, hold it cut-side down over a bowl and tap the skin firmly with a wooden spoon. The seeds and any juice should fall into the bowl.

Pomegranate molasses is made by boiling the juice down until it has a thick consistency similar to maple syrup. It's tart and sweet at the same time and the balance between the two will simply depend on the fruit used and how ripe it was at the time. The molasses enhances other flavours and can be used in both savoury and sweet dishes. I'm a big fan and tend to chuck it into dishes wherever I can – you'll find it in savoury recipes, sauces, marinades and salad dressings, but I'm just as likely to use it in desserts or blended with fruit in a cocktail or smoothie. Pomegranate molasses is now widely available – some bigger supermarkets even stock it, but you're more likely to find it in specialist shops. If you're going to be cooking food from this part of the world regularly, it's worth investing in a large bottle. I guarantee you'll be reaching for it as often as you do salt and pepper.

Pomegranate ketchup

When you want tomato ketchup with more sharpness and kick, use this. Utterly easy to mix up, and perfect on hamburgers. Mix two tablespoons tomato ketchup with 2 tablespoons pomegranate molasses and 2 tablespoons tomato purée, adding salt to taste.

Pulses

Second only to grains in terms of their importance in our diet are pulses – chickpeas, lentils and countless types of beans, both dried and fresh. If I'm looking for authenticity and wanting to recreate dishes as I enjoy them in Lebanon, then soaking and cooking dried pulses is essential, but frankly it's a time-consuming process and I don't always have that luxury. I've come up with a method for quick-soaking beans (see below) but tinned beans make a perfectly acceptable substitute and in terms of 'express' cooking, they're invaluable. If you've got a good selection of tins in your store cupboard you'll know you've always got a quick and easy meal on hand.

Pimping up tinned beans

I came up with this way to make tinned chickpeas taste better and, when they're prepared this way, they're a better tasting substitute for all types of bean. Take a 400g tin of beans in water, wash and drain them well then place in a saucepan with the juice of a lemon, a sliced clove of garlic and 1 teaspoon salt. Cover with water, bring to the boil then remove from the heat and leave to sit for 5 minutes. Drain well before use.

Quick-soaking beans

This method gives you pre-soaked beans in a couple of hours, so it's super fast and easy. The weight of beans slightly more than doubles as they soak, so 200g dried makes about 450g when soaked and drained. Wash the beans then tip into a saucepan, add water (to 3 times their depth), bring to the boil then simmer for 2–3 minutes. Turn the heat off, stir in 1 teaspoon bicarb (for every 400g dry beans), then place the lid on and leave for 2 hours. Drain, rinse then use as required. If cooked beans are needed, just return them to the saucepan, cover with fresh water then bring to the boil and simmer for 2–3 hours until soft.

Rose

Rose is a widely used flavouring in the Middle East and you'll come across it in sweets, desserts and pastries but also in savoury contexts, where it is dried and added to spice mixes or even stirred through rice dishes. Although you can use rose petals to flavour your dishes, rose water or essence is a more reliable and accurate means of adding the flavour as the strength can be measured and adjusted accordingly. Rose water is a clear, fragrant liquid distilled from wild rose petals. It's often used in combination with orange blossom water.

Saffron

This rare, expensive spice, believed to have first been grown in Iran, needs to be hand-picked from the crocus flower, and because there are so few stigmas on each flower, it takes a lot to make up even a tiny weight of saffron. You'll find it used in older recipes for pilaf but partly due to its cost and scarcity its less commonly used in Lebanese and Arab cookery today. For me, this is a shame so I try to use it often in recipes. The flavour is intense so you shouldn't need much when you're cooking. Try to dissolve the threads in warm water and let the liquid sit for 10–15 minutes for the colour and flavour of the spice to seep out. For an intense saffron sumac mayonnaise pour 1 tbsp boiling water on 12 threads of saffron, leave 10–15 minutes then beat into 150g thick mayonnaise with 1 tsp ground sumac.

Sumac

Sumac is a dark, deep-red coloured spice, made by crushing the dried red berries of the shrub of the same name. It has a sour astringent flavour, a little like lemon, and is used abundantly in our cooking. Sometimes a bowl of it is served alongside meals for diners to add their own.

Tabbouleh

The classic salad from the Levant. Essentially a parsley salad, made with lots of chopped parsley leaves and a little mint, then in decreasing amounts: chopped tomato, spring onion, uncooked washed bulgar wheat (never couscous), salt, pepper, lemon juice and olive oil. That's it. For me the bulgar wheat is never optional, I just wash it beforehand then let it soak up the juice from the tomato. Some people add hot green chilli, but that's not so traditional. Make it fresh, serve it fresh.

Tahini, or Tahina

Tahina or tahini are the same thing: a paste made by grinding sesame seeds. It is one of the main ingredients in a traditional hummus, but is found on the table at most meals in different guises – in its pure state, as a dressing or sauce (see below) or in pastries and desserts. I've even added it to shakes (page 270) to add richness and a fabulous thick, creamy backnote. The seeds can be toasted or germinated and ground whole, for a dark paste, or hulled, for a light shade and lighter flavour.

Tahini yoghurt sauce

Perfect as a substitute for mayonnaise, or for a simple yoghurt sauce. Just stir together 1 tablespoon of labneh (page 20) or thick Greek-style yoghurt with 1 teaspoon of tahini, 2 teaspoons of lemon juice and salt to taste. Thin with a little oil or water as needed.

Tomatoes

Really just go for the best tomatoes you can buy, firm but ripe. If a recipe needs a great-tasting tomato there's really no substitute. I like to make a Lebanese-style salsa by chopping 1 large tomato, 1 deseeded green chilli, half a red onion and a handful of fresh coriander leaves. Mix with the juice of a lemon, 4 tablespoons of olive oil, 2 tablespoons of pomegranate molasses and salt to taste.

Yoghurt

Look for live yoghurt or natural yoghurt as that will have the best flavour and texture. Low-fat is fine, but you might want to strain it over a cloth to make it slightly thicker (see Labneh, page 20). Greek yoghurt is slightly strained and full fat, and has a very rich flavour. Making your own is very easy. First wash your storage pot out with hot water and a sterilising solution (as you would a baby's bottle). Then pour enough milk to fill your container – either cow, goat or sheep's milk – into a saucepan and heat to 85°C to deactivate the protein so the yoghurt sets better. Then cool it to 43°C, stir in a few tablespoons of plain yoghurt, pour into your storage pot and leave in a warm place overnight. The next day stir it well then chill in the refrigerator for a day before using. It will be thinner than shop-bought but has a great bright flavour.

Za'atar

Za'atar can cause a little confusion. It's the term for the Middle Eastern spice mix made from a heady combination of herbs, spices and seeds; however, it's also the name of a herb itself. As with so much of Middle Eastern cooking, there are many regional variations. Its uses are limitless: it can be sprinkled over food on its own, stirred into dips or through rice, or massaged over chicken or meat as a dry rub. In Lebanon it's strongly associated with the breakfast table, where it's used in both a sweet and a savoury context. Although there are some good ready-prepared versions available, nothing really compares to making your own – it's so easy to do and you can adjust the levels of each flavour according to your own preferences. Our version at Comptoir is made by toasting ½ teaspoon of sesame seeds in a dry frying pan until just golden. Tip into a mortar and add ½ teaspoon of sumac and 1 teaspoon each of dried thyme, marjoram and oregano with a good pinch of sea salt. Pound with the pestle until everything is well ground. Store in an airtight container and use within a month.

9. Save those herb stalks, they are excellent added to the water towards the end when you simmer beans **10.** Cyprus potatoes have a golden flesh and a flaky skin, a little like jersey royals. My favourite potato for Lebanese cooking **11.** Look for firm unblemished okra, and use it as soon as you can if it's fresh. Frozen is good too **12.** Aubergines should have a smooth glossy skin, feel firm, but can vary in shape from bulbous to elongated. Experiment, you won't go wrong **13.** I use Baby Gem lettuce often, Cos lettuce as well, but iceberg almost never **14.** Radishes washed and chopped are excellent in salad-style mezze, and very good with dips **15.** We only lightly cook cauliflower, adding it to salads or simply frying it in small florets to serve with a tahini yoghurt sauce **16.** Vary your olives, don't just buy the purple sort. Look for tiny bronze ones, and the cracked bitter green sort, they have a fresher flavour **17.** Vine leaves cooked and packed in brine keep well in the cupboard.

Vegetables & Salads

CAULIFLOWER OLIVE FRITTERS 38

OKRA WITH FRESH CORIANDER 40

GRILLED AUBERGINE WITH A CUMIN & GARLIC RUB 42

GREEN BEANS WITH CHILLI TOMATOES 48

POTATO SALAD, THREE FLAVOURS 50

SPINACH FATAYER TRIANGLES 52

RED BABA GHANOUSH 56

SPICED PEPPER SALAD 58

SPICED STUFFED TOMATOES 60

WARM SALAD OF ARTICHOKES, BROAD BEANS & PEAS 64

TOMATO & SPRING ONION SALAD 66

BABY SPINACH SALAD, COMPTOIR-STYLE 68

AUBERGINE & HALLOUMI STACKS 70

Vegetables & Salads

In terms of 'express' food, the recipes in this chapter are about as fast as it gets, and when I'm thinking about how to get food on the table as quickly as possible, vegetables are often where it all begins; they're my building blocks. Aubergines are a favourite and I can generally rely on finding a few in the bottom of my fridge, so the starting point of a meal will often be a simple dish of grilled aubergines (page 42). From here, I'll add something a little more substantial. If it's just me, I might need nothing more than a Tomato and Spring Onion Salad (page 66) and some grilled halloumi, but if I'm cooking for friends, I might turn to a salad based on ingredients we use abundantly at Comptoir. The beauty of vegetable dishes and salads is that you can prepare them in large quantities and they'll keep well in the fridge. In fact the flavours will often improve the longer you leave them.

Cauliflower olive *fritters*

step by step

1. Break half a cauliflower into small florets **2.** Place in a pan with 1 chopped shallot and 100ml water, then put a lid on and bring to the boil. Simmer on a low heat for 2–3 minutes until tender then drain well. Chop the cauliflower roughly then mix with 30g chopped green olives and ½ teaspoon dried chilli flakes **3.** Tip 3 tablespoons plain flour into a bowl **4.** Beat in 1 large egg and 2 tablespoons milk until smooth **5.** Stir in a small handful of chopped parsley, 50g finely chopped halloumi and the cauliflower mixture then season well **6.** Heat a thin layer of oil in a frying pan over a medium heat. Spoon tablespoons of the mixture into the pan, spaced 3–4cm apart. Watch the heat so the fritters don't burn. As soon as they're almost set and golden underneath, flip over very carefully and fry the other side. Repeat with the remaining mixture. Serve sprinkled with salt.

Okra WITH fresh coriander

If you've never tried okra before, here's your chance. This recipe uses them whole, which leaves them deliciously tender and without that sometimes off-putting slimy texture that can occur when they're chopped or split before cooking.

SERVES 4

2 tbsp olive oil

1 large onion, finely sliced

1 garlic clove, sliced

1 tsp coriander seeds, crushed

100ml tomato purée

250ml hot vegetable stock

200g okra

handful of chopped coriander

salt and ground black pepper

Put the olive oil in a pan over a medium heat then fry the onion for about 10 minutes, until the onion is looking really golden.

Add the garlic, coriander seeds and tomato purée and mix it all together, then pour in the vegetable stock. Bring to the boil then reduce the heat and let everything simmer for around 15 minutes until the sauce has reduced and thickened slightly. Season with salt and pepper, to taste.

Blanch the okra in boiling water for a minute then drain and add to the tomato mix. Simmer for a few minutes more until the okra are barely tender, stir in the coriander and serve.

Grilled aubergine *with a* cumin & garlic rub

I love aubergines and I really love garlic so this recipe is a no-brainer for me. I'll happily devour a huge bowl of this for dinner with just some flatbread to scoop up the juices, but I'm just as likely to serve it to friends as part of a mezze. The flavours deepen the longer you leave it so it's great to make up a big batch and keep it in the fridge for when an emergency strikes. It will keep for about three days.

SERVES 4

1 tsp cumin seeds

1 garlic clove, sliced or crushed

3 tbsp olive oil

1 aubergine, sliced into rounds about 1cm thick

salt and ground black pepper

Heat the grill to its highest setting. Scatter the cumin seeds into a frying pan and toast for a minute or two until fragrant. Scrape into a bowl and stir in the garlic and olive oil. Season well.

Using a sharp knife, mark a criss-cross in the middle of the aubergine rounds on each side. Brush the spiced oil over the face of the rounds and grill under the hot grill until golden on each side.

MY SECRET
I'm quite addicted to fried garlic so here I would slice extra garlic and fry it in olive oil until it's golden and crisp, then sprinkle the garlic chips over the aubergines to serve.

Firmness is everything; dodge the soft ones and grab the ones that feel hard.

{ SKIN COLOUR VARIES }

so don't be put off by streaks of white, green or lavender.

Once cooked,

PRESERVE

by storing in oil in the fridge with slices of garlic and herbs – mezze on tap.

BEFORE COOKING:

to salt or not to salt? Today, most varieties aren't very bitter so you can skip this step.

ONCE COOKED, SPOON OUT THE FLESH THEN SALT IT AND PLACE IT IN A SIEVE TO DRAIN THE MOISTURE AND HELP DRY IT.

comptoir larder

aubergines

JUST BEFORE BAKING

prick aubergines to stop them exploding in the oven; there's no need to do this if grilling, however, as the side nearest to the heat bursts of its own accord.

WHEN YOU'VE GOT THE OVEN ON for something else, why not bake some aubergines until tender, then freeze or store in the fridge for another meal.

Store in the fridge

as the skin will wrinkle and the flesh will become bitter if left at room temperature.

IF THEY'RE FRESH THE SKIN WILL BE TAUT AND SHINY.

SHAPES VARY

from slender and long to small and egg-like.

GREEN *beans* with CHILLI tomatoes

This simple dish is found all over Lebanon. Recipes will vary widely according to the cook and the region but the staples are the beans, tomatoes, garlic and onions. It's a dish that relies on gently fusing flavours together until you have a soft, harmonious marriage so be careful to stick to the timings given below so that you achieve this. This is particularly important for the beans – they should be tender not squeaky.

SERVES 4

2 tbsp olive oil

1 red onion, chopped

1 garlic clove, crushed

½ tsp chilli flakes

1 tsp cumin seeds

3 tomatoes, chopped

2 tbsp pomegranate molasses

1 tbsp tomato purée

150ml hot vegetable stock

300g green beans

handful of chopped coriander

salt and ground black pepper

lemon wedges, to serve

Heat the oil in a large frying pan and gently fry the onion for 10–15 minutes until starting to soften and turn golden at the edges. Stir in the garlic, chilli and cumin and season well.

As soon as you can smell the aroma of the garlic, throw in the chopped tomatoes and any juices that have leached out on to the board. Add the pomegranate molasses and tomato purée, give everything a really good stir and pour in the vegetable stock. Cover, quickly turn the heat down really low and allow to simmer and cook for around 3–5 minutes so that the tomatoes become really saucy. Season well, to taste.

Take the lid off the pan and tuck the green beans into the sauce, pressing them down slightly with the back of a spoon. Cover again and cook for a good 8 minutes – the beans should be tender by the time they're done. Test them by slicing one through the middle. Stir in the coriander and serve with the lemon wedges.

potato salad, three flavours

Keep the potatoes whole when you cook them; that way you can chop them to exactly the size you want and you won't end up with any mushy bits at the end. For me, the key is to add the dressing while the potatoes are still warm so they absorb all the flavours.

SERVES 4

500g new potatoes

olive oil

either flavour 1

4 tbsp labneh

4 spring onions, chopped

1 tsp nigella seeds

1 garlic clove, peeled and mashed

or flavour 2

zest of 1 lemon

2 tbsp chopped dill

juice of ½ lemon

or flavour 3

2 garlic cloves, peeled and thinly sliced

1 tsp ground turmeric

1 tsp cumin seeds

good pinch of chilli flakes

good pinch of dried thyme

2 tbsp pomegranate molasses

2 tbsp chopped coriander

Bring a pan of salted water to the boil. Add the potatoes, bring back to the boil then cover and simmer for around 15 minutes until they are tender when you push a knife in. Drain well.

For the first two salads put all the flavouring ingredients into a bowl with 2–3 tablespoons of olive oil, seasoning well. Roughly chop the drained potatoes then add them to the bowl – I actually chop mine in the bowl with a knife. I try to keep the potatoes quite chunky but go for the texture you want.

For the third salad, put 2 tablespoons of olive oil into a frying pan with the garlic, turmeric, cumin, chilli and thyme and cook for a minute or two until the garlic starts to turn golden. Add the pomegranate molasses and roughly chopped potatoes, tossing them round until they're crisp and have absorbed all the spices. Stir the coriander through just before serving. Serve warm for the best flavour.

{ **MY SECRET**
I always cook more potatoes than I need, so I have them ready for another night. They're absolutely fine in the fridge for about three to five days once you put them in a lidded container. }

SPINACH *fatayer* triangles

If you eat fatayer in Lebanon, you'll notice that the dough they're made with is more bread-like than the pastry used here. Using a ready-made pastry will not only save you a lot of time it will make the casing crisp and moreish, while still retaining the essence of the dish. Here I've used a quick and simple spinach and halloumi stuffing, but you could experiment by adding chopped feta or mozzarella or by swapping the pine nuts for walnuts. Serve these warm with a couple of other salads or mezze dishes.

MAKES 18, ENOUGH TO SERVE 6–8

2 tbsp olive oil

1 onion

1 tsp ground coriander

½ tsp ground cumin

pinch of dried chilli flakes

1 garlic clove, sliced

2 tbsp pine nuts

2 tbsp sultanas

200g spinach leaves

50g halloumi, finely chopped

500g shortcrust pastry

plain flour, for dusting

1 large egg, beaten

sesame seeds

salt and ground black pepper

Pour the oil into a pan and heat gently while you chop the onion. Add the onion to the pan and cook gently for 10–12 minutes until it starts to turn golden. Season and stir in all the spices, garlic, pine nuts and sultanas. Stir well, allowing the pine nuts to turn golden in the heat of the pan.

If the spinach leaves are very large, roughly chop them, then add to the pan and clamp on a lid so that the steam wilts the spinach. Stir in the halloumi, season again then spoon the mixture into a bowl to cool.

Heat the oven to 200°C/180°C fan/gas 6.

Cut the pastry in half and roll one piece out with a little flour until it's about 2–3mm thick. Take a 9cm round bowl and put it on top of the pastry. Cut around it to make a circle then continue to do this, keeping as close to the last circle as you can, until you have eight circles. Re-roll the trimmings and cut out one more piece.

Drain the filling of any excess juice then put a teaspoon full onto each round, teasing it into a triangle, then brush egg around the exposed pastry. Bring the sides of the pastry up into a triangle shape and pinch them together, leaving a hole in the middle. Brush more egg over the outside of the pastry. Sprinkle with sesame seeds and a little salt. Put them on to a baking sheet then repeat with the other half of the pastry and filling to make 18 triangles. Bake in the oven for 20–25 minutes until golden. Cool until just warm and serve.

Red
baba ghanoush

This is my version of the traditional baba ghanoush, made with peppers as well as aubergines, to give it extra punch. If you're not a big fan of raw garlic, leave it out – it's delicious either way. Without the garlic the natural sweetness of the peppers shines through, whereas with it, the dish becomes wonderfully aromatic and punchy. Slices of toasted pitta bread are a must but it's so moreish I often find myself making a batch and serving it with griddled lamb, over a simple salad of spinach leaves or dolloped next to a simple piece of fish.

SERVES 4

1 aubergine

2 red peppers

1 garlic clove, crushed with a good pinch of salt

¼ tsp crumbled chilli

½ tsp ground coriander

good pinch of sumac

2 tbsp tomato purée

1 tbsp brown sugar

2 tbsp olive oil

juice of ½ lemon

1–2 tbsp tahini

salt

Turn the grill on to its highest setting and get it really hot. Put the aubergine and peppers on a baking sheet and grill until the skins have blackened. Check them regularly, turning them once each side is done.

Put the peppers and aubergine into a bowl and cover with cling film. Once the skins have loosened, peel them off then put the flesh into a blender with the garlic, chilli, coriander, sumac, tomato purée, sugar, olive oil, lemon juice and tahini. Give it a good whizz to blend everything together. Season with salt and taste to check it's just right, adding more of anything you feel it needs. Spoon into a bowl, sprinkle with a little more sumac, then serve.

Spiced
PEPPER salad

Bright, fresh and bursting with a rich fusion of spices, this simple salad is a backbone of my cooking and there's often a bowl of it to be found tucked away in my fridge. It's a great dish to serve alongside grilled meats or white fish.

SERVES 4–6

4 large peppers (a mix of red, green, yellow or orange)

1 tsp coriander seeds

1 tsp cumin seeds

6 allspice berries

few sprigs of thyme

2 garlic cloves, sliced

50ml olive oil

squeeze of lemon juice

small handful of chopped flat-leaf parsley and dill

salt

Turn the grill on high and get it really hot. Put the peppers on a baking sheet and grill until they've blistered and blackened. Immediately tip them into a bowl and cover – I use a pan lid or a baking sheet – and put to one side for the skins to steam off.

Meanwhile, toast the seeds and allspice berries in a pan until you can smell that musky aroma from the cumin. Very roughly crush, then tip into another bowl and add the thyme, garlic and olive oil and a good pinch of salt.

Put the peppers in a large sieve and rest it over a bowl. Peel the skins and ease the stalk and any seeds from the inside away. Slice the flesh and add to the spiced oil with any of the juices that have fallen into the bowl. If I have time, I put this aside in a cool place to marinate for a couple of hours – it allows the flavours to intensify but it's not vital.

Stir in the lemon juice then spoon into a serving bowl and scatter over the herbs. This keeps well in the fridge for up to four days.

spiced Stuffed tomatoes

This dish is a real melting pot of flavours and textures. Salty cheese sits alongside sweet sultanas while crunchy pine nuts mingle with soft couscous – it's always a popular dish when I serve it to friends. It's also really easy to adapt for bigger numbers so you can increase the quantities according to how many you're serving.

By all means use rice instead of the couscous if that's what you've got to hand – just remember you need to cook it in the stock after you've added it and you'll need to adjust the quantity accordingly. Follow the packet instructions for the timing and use at least twice the volume of liquid to the rice.

SERVES 4

4 extra large 'beef' tomatoes

3 tbsp olive oil

3 tbsp pine nuts

1 shallot, roughly chopped

1 garlic clove, roughly chopped

3 tbsp sultanas

150ml hot stock

50g couscous

handful of chopped flat-leaf parsley

100g halloumi, finely chopped

1 tsp Baharat Spice Mix (page 11) or ½ tsp ground cinnamon mixed with ½ tsp za'atar, or the same quantity of dried thyme mixed with sesame seeds

za'atar

salt and ground black pepper

Heat the oven to 200°C/180°C fan/gas 6.

Cut the tops off the tomatoes and spoon out the filling. You may need to loosen some of the bits with a sharp knife if they are tough to scoop out. Roughly chop the filling.

Pour 2 tablespoons of the oil into a pan and heat gently. Add the pine nuts and leave them to turn a pale golden – watch them carefully so they don't colour too much. Add the tomato filling, shallot and garlic. Quickly stir-fry for 2–3 minutes, then throw in the sultanas. Pour 100ml of the stock into the pan and as soon as it's bubbling, pour in the couscous and cook till it swells and absorbs all the liquid. Stir in the parsley and halloumi and season with salt, pepper and spice mix. Take care not to add too much – it should be fragrant, rather than overpowering.

Divide between the hollowed-out tomatoes and put in an ovenproof dish. Drizzle over the remaining stock and olive oil, sprinkle with za'atar and bake for 20–25 minutes until the tomatoes are tender.

COMBINE FINE UNCOOKED BULGAR WHEAT

WITH PARSLEY AND ALLOW THE GRAIN TO DRAW EXCESS WATER FROM THE FRESHLY WASHED HERB TO ABSORB ITS FLAVOUR AND DRY THE PARSLEY.

Comptoir Pesto

Purée herbs like thyme and mint in the blender with oil (add it slowly, to taste), season with salt then store in a sterilised jar in the fridge for up to 2 weeks for a ready-made flavour enhancer.

{ *Flavour oil or vinegar*: roughly chop leftover herbs and place them in OIL OR VINEGAR to use for cooking. }

MINT, PARSLEY & CORIANDER

can be dried easily in a cooling oven (heat the oven on its lowest setting for a while then turn it off, pop in the herbs and leave to dry), then broken into crumbs and sprinkled on dishes before serving for a tea-like flavour.

Make a simple HERB BUTTER

by mixing chopped herbs with sumac and soft butter till smooth, then use it for grilling meat, fish and vegetables, basting them with the butter as they cook.

comptoir larder

herbs

Simple bread dough CAN BE TRANSFORMED BY MIXING IN LEFTOVER HERBS. JUST CHOP AND ADD THEM WITH THE LIQUID.

Plant small pots **of herbs** *in the garden as they'll grow better and yield more than on the windowsill.*

LEBANESE THYME
HAS SOFTER, LONGER LEAVES AND A MORE COMPLEX FLAVOUR THAN THE COMMON GARDEN KIND AVAILABLE IN THE UK. *Just substitute it in recipes in the same quantity.*

LIKE CUT FLOWERS, *fresh herbs benefit from having their stalk end re-cut before being placed in cold water to freshen the leaves.*

{ BEFORE ROASTING MEAT *or fish, rub the flesh with yoghurt, salt and crushed garlic then smother it with chopped herbs – they will crisp in the oven and release flavour.* }

Warm salad of artichokes, broad beans & PEAS

I can imagine lots of people might not be very comfortable with the idea of 'cooking' lettuce but it really does work. True, lettuce is fabulous when it's crisp, crunchy and coated in dressing, but adding a little heat to it just gives it another dimension. You could use hardier leaves, such as spinach or Swiss chard but that would change the texture and essence of the dish. Lettuce is sweet and soft and gives this salad a light, spring-like feel. And in true 'Express' style, it cooks much faster than its tougher winter equivalents. This salad is a cinch to construct, especially now it's getting easier to buy jars or tins of artichoke hearts.

SERVES 4

2 tbsp olive oil

bunch of spring onions, roughly chopped

1 tsp ground coriander

1 mild green chilli, chopped

2 garlic cloves, sliced

6 artichoke hearts from a tin or jar, drained well and halved

200g fresh broad beans, podded

200g fresh peas (or defrosted frozen peas if fresh are unavailable)

2 Little Gem lettuces, cut into wedges

handful of chopped dill

juice of ½ lemon

2 tbsp extra virgin olive oil

salt and ground black pepper

thick yoghurt, to serve

Heat the olive oil with plenty of seasoning in a pan over a medium heat and gently fry the spring onion until soft and slippery and starting to caramelise and turn golden.

Stir the coriander, chilli and garlic into the pan, mixing well. Allow the garlic to colour just a little, then stir in the artichoke hearts, broad beans and peas. Season again, add a good splash of water and cover with a lid immediately so that the vegetables steam in the water. This will take around 5 minutes.

Stir in the lettuce and dill, allowing the lettuce to wilt in the pan. Whisk together the lemon juice and olive oil and pour that over the top. Taste and add a splash more olive oil if you think it needs it. Spoon all the vegetables and lovely juices into a bowl and serve with a dollop of yoghurt on top.

Tomato & SPRING ONION salad

Dishes that are as simple as this one rely on the quality of your ingredients. I can tell you that there's no point making this salad in the depths of winter, when tomatoes will be hard and tasteless, flown into the UK from the other side of the world or forced to ripen under false conditions. Make this in the warmer months when soft ripe tomatoes burst with juices, and the Mediterranean flavours of the dish can combine in a magnificent summer medley.

SERVES 4

3 tbsp extra virgin olive oil

juice of 1 lemon

handful of chopped mint

small handful of chopped flat-leaf parsley

¼ cucumber

4 large tomatoes, quartered

10 cherry tomatoes, halved

4 spring onions, roughly chopped

salt

Take a large salad bowl and pour in the oil, lemon juice and herbs. Stir them all together and season with a good pinch of salt.

Halve then quarter the cucumber and cut off the wet seeds in the middle so you're just left with the firm part. Roughly chop this.

Add all the remaining ingredients to the bowl and mix everything well. Cover and set aside in a cool place in the kitchen for at least an hour until you're ready to serve.

MY SECRET

For a warm salad, halve all the tomatoes and chop the spring onions, roughly separating the white from the green. Cut the cucumber into chunks. Put on a baking sheet, brush with oil and season. Grill until golden and the veg have softened. Spoon into a bowl, sprinkle with the herbs, olive oil and lemon juice then crumble over a little feta.

Baby SPINACH salad, Comptoir-style

Lots of restaurants have a 'signature dish' – something that's permanently on their menu. It might be a dish that best sums up the ethos of the restaurant's cooking or simply one they know is popular with customers. At Comptoir our menu is constantly changing and evolving so while we don't have a signature dish as such, we do have signature ingredients – pillars of Lebanese cooking that we continually turn to. Similarly, I'll always have pitta breads, pine nuts, cumin and sumac in my cupboard and there will generally be some sort of salty cheese – either feta or halloumi – in the fridge. This salad is the punchy conclusion of flinging them together. All I need to do is pick up a few fresh items on my way home from work and I've got a vibrant, impressive salad with very little fuss.

SERVES 4

zest and juice of ½ large lemon

25g sultanas

2 pitta breads

1 tbsp olive oil

25g pine nuts

1 tsp sumac

½ tsp ground cumin

3 tbsp extra virgin olive oil

200g baby spinach

seeds of 1 small pomegranate or a handful of pitted chopped cherries

100g feta cheese, crumbled

salt

Put the lemon zest and juice in a bowl, add the sultanas, stir and put them to one side to plump up a little bit.

Grill the pitta breads until toasted, crisp and really golden.

Meanwhile, heat the olive oil in a pan, add the pine nuts, sumac and cumin and stir everything together until the pine nuts are golden. Break up the pitta and stir into this mixture so the pieces are all coated in the spiced oil.

Whisk the extra virgin olive oil into the sultanas and lemon juice and stir in a good pinch of salt.

Now it's time to assemble. Roughly chop the spinach, so the leaves are a bit easier to eat, then put into a large bowl. Spoon the pomegranate seeds over the top then add the feta, the pine nut mixture and finally drizzle over the dressing. Toss everything together and you're ready to eat.

AUBERGINE &
halloumi *stacks*

The great thing about these baked vegetable stacks is that they stay extra soft inside but go crisp at the edges, holding all the flavour and juice in the centre. Rinsing the grated halloumi reduces the saltiness so that it doesn't overly dominate. If you can't get halloumi then another melting cheese like mozzarella works well too. This is hugely rich, so just a couple per person will be enough when served with grilled meats or fish. Grilling or frying the aubergine slices in advance – just keep them in the fridge – means you can make these in a flash.

MAKES 8–10 STACKS

3–4 aubergines, sliced into rounds

2 tbsp olive oil, plus extra for brushing the aubergines

175g grated halloumi, rinsed and squeezed dry

6–8 tomatoes, sliced into rounds

small bunch of fresh herbs, such as mint, parsley or basil

2 chunky garlic cloves, peeled and thinly sliced

Heat an overhead grill or griddle until very hot. Lightly brush the aubergine slices with olive oil then grill or griddle until soft – about 2 minutes on each side.

Line a tray with non-stick baking paper. Heat the oven to 200°C/180°C fan/gas 6.

Layer the stacks with 3 aubergine slices, some grated halloumi, 2 tomato slices and a pinch of herbs in between each layer. Place the stacks on the tray, stick a toothpick through each centre to keep them upright then either cover and keep in the fridge until you're ready to cook them (they'll be fine for 2–3 days) or bake for 20–25 minutes, until hot and sizzling. While they're baking, heat the olive oil in a small pan and fry the garlic slices until golden. Place a few slices on top of each stack to serve.

Meat & Fish

Meat & Fish

Lebanon's extensive coastline means that there's an abundance of fresh fish in the region and it makes up a significant part of the Lebanese diet, though there's no doubt that the Lebanese also enjoy their meat. Unlike the extensive quantities that seem to be consumed in the UK, however, meat is used sparingly and carefully – a small quantity will be stretched to provide a filling meal. The recipes in this chapter embrace and reflect this tradition, while also staying true to an 'express' style of cooking. Offal may not be as popular with British cooks as with their Arab counterparts, but I've not shied from taking up the Lebanese mantle and have boldly given you not one but two recipes using liver – chicken and lamb's. If you're not familiar with liver, I really want you to give it a shot. It cooks in a flash, and the meltingly soft texture and rich, meaty flavour is just delicious.

Fish & POTATO kibbeh

Kibbeh are widely considered Lebanon's national dish. Usually torpedo-shaped croquettes with a minced meat and bulgar wheat crust filled with meat and spices. But the basic concept has been adapted and kibbeh come in many different shapes and guises. I've come up with this fishy version, which is far quicker and less fiddly to make. Using potato instead of bulgar as the binding element keeps the croquettes sturdy and robust, ensuring they won't fall apart when you fry them (though make sure the potato is very dry otherwise the moisture will prevent that). These kibbeh are best served warm with something crunchy and fresh – I usually serve them with a French-style carrot salad.

MAKES ABOUT 26, ENOUGH TO FEED 4 AS A MEZZE

4 spring onions, roughly chopped

1 green chilli, deseeded and roughly chopped

200g cooked white fish (haddock, cod or pollack), cooled

200g mashed potatoes

1 tsp ground coriander, plus a little extra to serve

small handful of chopped flat-leaf parsley and coriander

1 tsp Baharat Spice Mix (page 11) (optional)

olive oil, for frying

plain flour, for dusting

salt and ground black pepper

Put the spring onions, chilli, fish, potato and ground coriander in a food processor.

Whizz to mince everything together, then spoon into a bowl. Stir in the fresh herbs, the Baharat, if you're opting for it, and season with a good pinch of salt.

Spoon a couple of tablespoons of flour into a flat dish and season well.

Take two teaspoons and scoop up some of the mixture with one spoon then scrape it against the other to shape into a rough oval. Do it one more time to smooth the other side. Roll the kibbeh in the flour so that each side is coated. Continue to make all the ovals until you've used up all the mixture.

Pour a couple of millimetres of oil into a large frying pan and place over a medium heat. Line a baking tray or large plate with kitchen paper.

To check the oil is hot enough to start frying, drop a pinch of flour into it – if it sizzles you're ready.

Carefully lower three or four of the kibbeh into the hot oil and fry until golden on each side, then remove and place on the kitchen paper to soak up any excess oil. Sprinkle with salt and a little extra ground coriander and eat while still warm.

Grilled RED MULLET with *chilli sauce* & *yoghurt*

The warm Mediterranean waters are home to loads of different fish species, with red mullet, sea bass and sole being the most popular on the Lebanese coastline. Whole fish, rather than fillets, are often used there, because cooking on the bone, with the skin still protecting the flesh, means the fish is less likely to dry out. There's certainly no danger of that here, where the spicy marinade, made with olive oil, keeps the fish fillets deliciously moist. Serve the mullet with a simple green veg dish and some rice if you want to bulk it out.

SERVES 4

2 garlic cloves

1 green chilli, halved and deseeded

1 red chilli

2 tsp cumin seeds

zest and juice of 1 lemon

4 tbsp olive oil

4 small red mullet fillets (about 150g) or 2 large whole mullet

150ml thick yoghurt

1 tbsp chilli sauce

salt and ground black pepper

Put the garlic cloves on a board, place a large sharp knife on top and press down with the heel of your hand to crush. Peel away the skin.

Finely chop the chillies with the garlic on the board until they're minced, adding the cumin seeds for the last few chops.

Scrape all the paste off the board and into a shallow dish. Add the lemon zest and juice, then stir in the oil and season well. Brush all over the fish.

Heat the grill until hot. If using fillets, grill the fish for 4–5 minutes skin-side down until cooked through. If using whole fish you'll need to flip them and cook the other side. To check the fish is cooked, insert a sharp knife into the middle of the fish – the flesh should come away from the skin easily.

Whisk the yoghurt in a bowl with 1–2 tablespoons of cold water until smooth, then swirl in the chilli sauce and serve with the fish.

MY SECRET

If you can't get hold of red mullet or would prefer to use a fish that's fished in British waters, fillets of pollack, line-caught cod or haddock would also work well here.

Seabass *with date purée*

step by step

1. Put 12 pitted dates in a bowl, cover with boiling water, leave to soften for 30 minutes then drain, reserving the liquid *2.* Put in a mini food processor with 1 teaspoon ground cinnamon, ½ teaspoon allspice, a good pinch of chilli flakes. Whizz to a purée, adding a teaspoon or two of the soaking liquid if very thick *3.* Spoon into a bowl and stir in 1–2 tablespoons pine nuts *4.* Lay 8 sea bass fillets, skin-side down, on a board. Season then grate over some lemon zest. Spread the date paste over four fillets *5.* Cover with the remaining fillets and dust both sides of the fish sandwiches with flour and season again *6.* Heat about 1½ teaspoons of oil in a frying pan and fry the sandwiched fish in batches for 3–4 minutes on one side until golden and crisp, then carefully turn over and fry the other side until cooked through. Repeat with the remaining fish sandwiches, adding extra oil if needed. Serve with lemon wedges.

Lebanese spiced squid

Here I've created a Lebanese twist on the classic fried calamari dish – deep-fried squid coated in a light batter. For simplicity's sake I've opted to shallow- rather than deep-fry the squid but the result is just as good. Make sure you use cornflour rather than plain flour – it keeps the coating really light and crispy.

SERVES 4

50g cornflour

1 tbsp ground coriander

1½ tsp cayenne pepper

2 teaspoons ground cumin

1 tsp ground allspice

1 tsp salt

½ tsp freshly ground black pepper

700g squid, cleaned

vegetable oil, for frying

Measure the cornflour and spices into a sealable container, then add the salt and pepper. Cut the squid into rough rectangles, each about 3 x 5cm. Score one side in a criss-cross pattern. Drop the squid into the container, put the lid on then give it a good shake. If you don't have a container, use a large bowl and put a plate on top.

Pour enough oil into a pan until it's a couple of centimetres deep. Heat the oil over a medium heat until it's hot. You can check it's ready by dropping a pinch of flour into it – it should sizzle madly. Cover a baking tray with a couple of sheets of kitchen paper.

Lower the squid carefully into the hot oil, cooking three or four pieces at a time. Depending on how thick each piece is, they'll take no more than 30–40 seconds in total. Flip them over once they're golden on one side and cook until they have an even colour all over. Lift out with a slotted spoon and sprinkle with salt to serve.

MY SECRET
For a delicious sauce finely chop 1 large tomato, 1 seeded green chilli, half a red onion and a handful of fresh coriander leaves. Add the juice of a lemon, 4 tbsp olive oil, 2 tbsp pomegranate molasses and salt to taste.

Chilli-spiced chicken livers *with* quick garlic sauce

If chicken livers aren't yet one of your fridge staples, I'm hoping I can change that, because where fast food is concerned, chicken livers are one of your best friends. They cook in under 10 minutes – need I say more – and their rich, irony meatiness stands up well to other strong flavours. Here I've gone for a spicy version using chilli, but in Lebanon they're very often served in a sweeter context. Although liver does need to be cooked properly, it's best served lightly caramelised on the outside but still rosy in the middle.

SERVES 2–4

1 garlic clove, peeled

1 red chilli

400g chicken livers

1 tbsp olive oil

½ tsp ground allspice

small handful of chopped flat-leaf parsley

sumac

salt and ground black pepper

for the quick garlic sauce

2 garlic cloves

1 tbsp olive oil

2 tbsp thick yoghurt or labneh

1 lemon

Start with the garlic sauce. Put the garlic cloves on a board, place a large, sharp knife on top and use the heel of your hand to press down and crush them. The skin will come off instantly and you'll be left with two squashed cloves. Place in a food processor with the oil, yoghurt and a good squeeze of lemon juice and whizz to combine. Season with salt and put to one side.

Now move on to the chicken livers. Slice the garlic and the chilli, removing any seeds if you prefer less heat. Check the livers and snip them in two if they're hanging in pairs, discarding the fatty bits and sinew.

Heat the oil in a large frying pan and stir in the garlic and chilli. Add the chicken livers and allspice and season well. Allow the livers to cook on one side for a good 3 minutes until they've caramelised, then flip each piece over and cook for 2–3 minutes more on the other side.

Stir in the parsley and a good pinch of sumac and serve with the garlic sauce drizzled over the top.

{ **PERK UP** *leftover* **meat** by heating it gently then top with a layer of dip and chopped roasted nuts. }

Meat becomes more tender and flavoursome if left in a simple marinade for 2–3 hours before cooking. Use a little acid, like vinegar or lemon juice, with garlic, salt and sugar rubbed well in for the best result.

Freeze cubes of **LAMB** or **BEEF** TO MAKE KEBABS. COAT THEM IN YOGHURT BEFORE FREEZING AS THIS WILL MAKE THEM MORE TENDER WHEN YOU THAW THEN GRILL THEM.

Your fishmonger has the skills – use them: ask them to clean, fillet and trim the whole fish for you.

If you can't get enough of one sort of meat or fish for everyone's main course, serve it mezze-style. Starter-sized portions of meat and fish will serve many more alongside flatbreads, dips and salads.

comptoir larder

meat & fish

COMPARE THE PRICES of cuts of meat on and off the bone; today the best value isn't always the least prepared.

Fish will keep slightly longer IN THE FRIDGE IF FILLETED AND PLACED IN AN ACIDIC MARINADE – HELPFUL IF YOU HAVE TO POSTPONE THAT DINNER PLAN FOR A DAY.

SPICE IT:

If you like your meat hot, brush it with a little diluted harissa before grilling as it will char slightly in the heat giving a smoky hot flavour.

If fish or meat is going off, long cooking and spices won't save it – that's a myth. Sadly you have to throw it away.

FRESH FISH should feel fairly firm and have a briny, salty aroma.

Chicken express, *Comptoir-style*

Middle Eastern dining is a very sociable affair – it's about sharing food and mixing up dishes so that everyone can have a little of what they want. Generally there will be hot and cold, sweet and spicy, crunchy and creamy on the table and you can take as much or as little of each to create your own meal. This dish is inspired by that ethos. I would serve it as part of a mezze selection, alongside lots of salads, dips and flatbreads, but if you're after a quick supper for two, it would work equally well served simply with some rice and a hot vegetable dish such as the Okra with Fresh Coriander (page 40).

SERVES 2–4

1 tsp cumin seeds

1 tsp ground coriander

¼ tsp dried chilli flakes

3 tbsp olive oil

½ lemon

2 x 150g skinless, boneless chicken breasts

salt and ground black pepper

Heat the cumin seeds in a pan for about 30 seconds until toasted. Tip into a bowl and add the coriander, chilli and olive oil. Grate the zest of the lemon over the top and season well.

Put the chicken on a board and open it out so that the fillet on the inside is stretched out too. Slice each breast lengthways into thin, finger-width lengths. Drop into the bowl of spiced oil and stir everything together.

Heat a large frying pan until hot – there's no need to add any oil as the chicken is marinated in plenty. Slip one piece of chicken in to check the pan is hot enough. If it sizzles, it's ready. Slide in the rest of the chicken and cook over a medium high heat until one side is golden. It will take 2–3 minutes. Flip the chicken over when you see a clean white edge appearing around each piece. Continue to cook on the other side for 2–3 minutes. Check it's cooked by slicing a piece in half and making sure there aren't any pink juices.

MY SECRET

You can make either just the spiced oil or marinate the chicken up to a day ahead if you want to. If you are marinating it, just make sure you keep the chicken in a sealed container and take it out of the fridge about 30 minutes before you're going to cook it to allow it to come to room temperature.

Lamb chop & red lentil stew

One-pot cooking is less fussy than having lots of separate pans on the heat and, more importantly, it allows the meat or fish to take on the aromas of the herbs and spices, while infusing the cooking liquid with flavour. It's a homely and hearty style of cooking. So when I want something soothing yet filling this warming stew is often the one I fling together. With the chops, vegetables and lentils, it can be a meal in itself, though to really up the comfort factor I like to serve it with couscous to soak up all the rich, meaty juices.

SERVES 4

1 onion, chopped

1 red pepper, chopped

1 aubergine, chopped

1 courgette, chopped

2 tbsp olive oil

4 garlic cloves, sliced

½ tsp dried chilli flakes

sprig of rosemary

1 tsp ground coriander

100g red lentils

about 400ml hot lamb stock

1 tbsp tomato purée

4 lamb chops

salt and ground black pepper

Put the onion, pepper, aubergine and courgette into a pan with the oil. Season well and cook over a medium heat, stirring every now and then for about 10 minutes. By this stage the vegetables will be turning golden and caramelised.

Sprinkle over the garlic, chilli, rosemary and coriander and stir in along with the red lentils. Pour the stock over the top then stir in the tomato purée. Tuck the lamb chops into the pan, pushing them underneath the stock. Season again.

Cover the pan with a lid, bring to the boil then turn the heat down low and cook for around 50 minutes or until the chops are tender, adding more stock during the cooking if you think it needs more liquid.

One-pot fast roast chicken

When I first arrived in London, I was fascinated by British food – it was worlds apart from the flavours I knew and loved. And over 25 years later that fascination continues. I've learned so much about British culture and I've developed a respect for its traditions and, dare I say it, 'quirks'. One aspect that continues to intrigue me is the British devotion to their Sunday roast. I love a traditional roast chicken but the reason it's called a 'Sunday roast' is evident in the cooking time – you need a lazy Sunday morning for your bird to cook gently and slowly. So I wanted to see if I could tweak the concept, speed it up, and of course, in a nod to my roots, spice it up too. This is the result – the chicken takes 5 minutes to prepare and just under an hour to cook, and to me it's the perfect melding of my heritage and my new home.

SERVES 4–6

1 tsp cayenne pepper

½ tsp ground cinnamon

1 tsp ground cumin

1 tsp ground coriander

zest of 1 lemon

3 tbsp olive oil, plus a little extra

1 large onion, thickly sliced

2 large potatoes, thickly sliced

1 chicken

salt and ground black pepper

Heat the oven to 220°C/200°C fan/gas 7.

Mix all the spices, lemon zest and oil in a bowl. Put the onion and potatoes into a large roasting tin.

Put the chicken on a board, breast-side down. Feel along the edge of each side of the backbone where the ribs begin and score down each side with a sharp knife. Take a pair of sharp kitchen scissors and cut along each side to remove the backbone.

Turn the chicken over and press the heel of your hand in the middle of the breastbone to flatten it out. Lay the flattened chicken on top of the potato and onion mixture and pour the spiced oil all over. Season well. Pour 200ml water around the chicken and drizzle a little more olive oil over the potatoes.

Roast in the oven for 10 minutes, then turn it down to 200°C/180°C fan/gas 6. Continue to roast for 40–45 minutes. Check the chicken is ready by pushing a sharp knife into the thigh – the juices should run clear.

Spiced & crumbed
fried CHICKEN

Chicken nuggets, Comptoir style. I've used a yoghurt marinade to keep the chicken moist and give a tangy flavour. I've spiced up the crumbed exterior with a mixture of sweet (cinnamon), hot (cayenne pepper) and slightly sour (sumac) spices. The secret to fried chicken is a really crisp coating but you also need to make sure the chicken is thoroughly cooked through. When shallow-frying the chicken, as I've done here, you need to place it over a high heat to brown the crumb then turn the heat down to cook the chicken. It's delicious served plain but you could also serve it with the Quick Garlic Sauce (page 86), which is a cool complement to the spiced coating, or with a saffron sumac mayonnaise (page 25).

SERVES 4

4 tbsp thick yoghurt

2 tbsp olive oil

zest and juice of ½ lemon

4 x 150g skinless, boneless chicken breasts or thighs, cut into bite-sized chunks

vegetable oil, for frying

1 medium egg, beaten

salt and ground black pepper

for the spiced crumbs

2 tsp ground cinnamon

2 tsp cayenne pepper

2 tsp garlic salt

1 tsp sumac

½ tsp ground allspice

2 tbsp plain flour

3 slices of white bread

Put the yoghurt, oil, lemon zest and juice in a bowl and season well. Drop the chicken pieces into the bowl, stir well and set aside.

Put all the ingredients for the spiced crumb into a food processor, roughly tearing up the slices of bread as you put them in. Whizz to make a fine crumb mixture, then tip into a shallow dish.

Pour a couple of centimetres of oil into a large pan and place over a medium heat. Cover a baking tray with kitchen paper.

Pour the beaten egg over the chicken and stir well to coat all the pieces. Spoon four or five pieces of chicken into the spiced crumb and toss to coat. Check the oil is ready by dropping a pinch of flour into it – it should sizzle madly – then carefully lower the coated chicken into the hot oil. You may need to turn the heat right down at this stage so the chicken doesn't brown too quickly on the outside. Cook for about 1½ minutes, then turn over and cook the other side for the same time.

Lift out and drain on the kitchen paper, then sprinkle with salt, and continue to cook the chicken in batches until it's all cooked.

Comptoir fried chicken

A long way from Kentucky but even more delicious. Serve this with shoestring fries tossed with salt and za'atar, boiled corn on the cob with Pomegranate Hot Sauce (page 204) and my take on baked beans (see below) for a complete feast.

SERVES 4

4 tbsp thick yoghurt

2 tbsp olive oil

zest and juice of ½ lemon

8–12 chicken drumsticks or thighs, or a mix of both

vegetable oil, for frying

salt and ground black pepper

for the dipping batter

1 egg

2 tbsp pomegranate molasses

250ml cold water

175g plain flour

for the spice coating

350g plain flour

1 tsp ground cinnamon

3 tsp ground cumin

3 tsp garlic powder

3 tsp ground coriander

5 tsp dried mint

1 tsp chilli powder

2 tsp salt

Put the yoghurt, oil, lemon zest and juice in a bowl and season well. Drop the chicken into the bowl, stir well and set aside. Ideally do this a few hours before you want to fry the chicken.

Make the dipping batter by beating the egg, molasses, water and flour until smooth. For the spice coating simply mix everything together.

Heat enough oil in a heavy-based saucepan to fill it by a third (no more as it will bubble up) allowing enough room to fry two or three pieces of chicken at a time. You want the oil temperature at 175°C, so that when you drop in a cube of bread it browns and is fried in 2 minutes.

Dip the chicken pieces in the batter then in the spice coating in batches, then place in the hot oil with tongs. Fry the chicken for about 5–10 minutes until it's a deep golden brown and cooked through. Drain on kitchen paper and keep hot in the oven heated to 120°C/110°C fan/gas 1 while you fry the rest.

MY SECRET

For my take on baked beans you need 700g soaked and cooked fava or kidney beans, drained then mixed with 150g tomato ketchup, 50g brown sugar, 1 mashed garlic clove, 100g pomegranate molasses and 1 tsp salt. Bring to the boil and simmer for a minute before serving.

Lamb's liver with pomegranate & mint

In England, lamb's liver is most commonly served with fried onions, bacon and mash. The Scots bind it with oatmeal, salt and onions to make haggis, while the Lebanese often partner it with sweetness; here with pomegranate. The point I'm trying to make is that liver is an incredibly versatile ingredient, and happily, a cheap one too. It's a staple for me and I hope I can make it one for you too.

SERVES 4

400g lamb's liver

1 tsp dried mint

1 tbsp pomegranate molasses

2 tbsp olive oil

1 onion, sliced

2 garlic cloves, sliced

½ pomegranate

small handful of chopped mint

salt and ground black pepper

lemon wedges, to serve

thick yoghurt, to serve

Trim the liver of any lobes, then put into a bowl with the mint, pomegranate molasses and a drizzle of the olive oil. Give it a good season, stir then set aside.

Put the remaining oil and onion in a large frying pan over a medium heat. Give the pan a good shake to toss the onion around and cook for 5–8 minutes until it starts to caramelise.

Add the garlic to the pan and cook for a minute or so, then slide the marinated liver into the pan. Turn the heat up to medium high and cook for a couple of minutes until browned on one side, then stir everything well to turn the pieces over and cook the other side. Take care not to overcook the liver otherwise it will be tough.

Holding the pomegranate above the pan, bash it lightly with the back of a wooden spoon to release the seeds, then stir in the mint.

Serve the liver with the lemon wedges and a dollop of yoghurt on the side.

MY SECRET

Great served with spiced walnut rice pilaf. Place 400ml rice (by volume) in a pan with 700ml water, 1 teaspoon salt, 2 teaspoons sumac, 2 teaspoons sweet paprika, 1 teaspoon Baharat Spice and 3 tablespoons of tomato purée. Whisk everything well, add 100g chopped walnuts and bring to the boil. Cover and cook over a very low heat, allowing the rice to steam for 10–12 minutes or until all the liquid has been absorbed. Fluff with a fork to serve.

Comptoir *mixed* grill

Even if the meat you buy is of the most basic quality, a simple marinade gives the flavour a huge kick upward. Here I've added tomato and spices so they char very slightly over the flames. Easy, quick and one of my favourite ways to supercharge grilled meats.

SERVES 4

4 large tomatoes, halved horizontally

4 large flat mushrooms

za'atar (optional)

2 beef or lamb sausages

4 chicken drumsticks

4 lamb cutlets

2 small pieces steak (ribeye or sirloin are ideal)

salt and ground black pepper

Quick Pickled Cabbage (page 206), to serve

boiled rice, to serve

for the barbecue sauce

6 tbsp tomato purée

2 tsp ground coriander

1 tsp ground cumin

1 tsp cayenne pepper

1 tsp sumac

zest of ½ lemon

2 tbsp red wine vinegar

1 tbsp olive oil

1 tbsp pomegranate molasses

Heat the oven to 180°C/160°C fan/gas 4. Mix together all the ingredients for the barbecue sauce, seasoning well.

Brush the sauce liberally over the outside of the tomatoes, followed by the inside of the mushrooms, adding a sprinkling of za'atar if you like, then slather the sauce all over the steak and lamb cutlets.

Pinch each sausage in the middle and twist to make four smaller, thick and chunky sausages, then snip the joins. Place the sausages and chicken in an ovenproof dish, spoon some sauce over then cover with foil and bake for 40 minutes until cooked. This pre-cooking makes the final grilling a cinch.

Heat the grill to high or prepare your barbecue. Start by cooking the lamb cutlets. After a few minutes add the steak, tomatoes and mushrooms (I sit them on foil to hold the juices), then add the chicken and sausages and let them crisp. Season everything and check it's cooked properly before serving with rice and the quick pickled cabbage.

Eggs

COMPTOIR
LIBANAIS

Eggs

Not only are eggs plentiful in the Middle East, they are versatile and inexpensive and thus a mainstay of Lebanese cooking, making an appearance in different forms at most times of the day. Omelettes, fried and scrambled eggs are common sights on the breakfast table, though as you'll discover from the recipes here, the addition of traditional spice mixes, such as za'atar and sumac, means they're a punchier proposal than the European versions we're more familiar with in Britain. Get the best eggs you can afford, and treat them as a special ingredient in the kitchen. At its best, a fresh egg from a chicken that has eaten a good diet is one of the most delicious meals out there.

Lebanese scrambled eggs

How you like your eggs can be quite a divisive issue, and debates around runny versus set yolks or 'sunny-side up' versus cooked on both sides ('over easy' if you're American) can rage. So I know I'm being fairly bold in suggesting that anybody steps away from their preference and dips their toe (or their soldiers) into a different interpretation. I'm confident that this gently spiced scrambled egg will enlist converts. Serve on pitta bread rather than toast for a true Lebanese homage to a breakfast classic.

SERVES 4

2 large tomatoes, halved horizontally

big knob of butter

1 red chilli, chopped

1 tsp ground cumin

6 large eggs

small handful of chopped flat-leaf parsley

salt and ground black pepper

pitta bread, toasted, to serve

Heat the grill on a medium setting. Season the tomatoes well, and grill, cut-side up, until golden.

While the tomatoes are cooking, put the butter, chilli and cumin in a saucepan then put the pan over a medium heat. Allow the butter to melt, tilting the pan every now and then to move the chilli and cumin around in the melted butter.

Season well then stir in the eggs. Beat the eggs with a wooden spoon until they're well mixed, then continue to stir them over the heat as they cook to scramble them. When they're almost set, stir in half the parsley.

Divide among four plates, put half a tomato on the side, scatter with the remaining parsley and serve with the pitta or directly on top of it.

Fried eggs *with* cumin-spiced fried onions *& pitta*

We use onions a lot in our cooking at Comptoir but here they're made the star, served alongside simple fried eggs spiced up with cumin and chilli together with a stack of pitta. I like to serve this with a bowl of tahini sauce, made by mixing 100g thick yoghurt with 2 tablespoons tahini until smooth. Comforting food that's equally good for breakfast or a quick evening meal.

SERVES 1 OR 2

1 onion, sliced

2 tbsp olive oil, plus extra to fry the eggs

½ teaspoon cumin seeds

good sprinkle of chilli flakes

2–4 medium eggs, depending on how hungry you are

pitta bread, to serve

small handful of chopped flat-leaf parsley

salt

Put the onion and olive oil in a large frying pan and place over a medium heat. Cook for around 5 minutes, tossing the onions every now and then, until they're just starting to turn golden at the tips. This is the point where you need to watch them carefully otherwise they'll burn, so turn the heat down a little. Stir in the cumin seeds and chilli flakes and about 2 tablespoons of water. Continue to cook for a couple more minutes until the onion softens then season well.

Nudge the onions to the edge of the pan and drizzle in a little more oil if necessary to fry the eggs. Break in the eggs and cook until the whites are set. Put a lid on the pan at this point so that the egg yolks cook, without the need to add any more oil. You can sprinkle extra chilli and cumin over the eggs to spice them as well.

Toast or bake the pitta until it just starts to crisp then spoon the eggs on to the plate with the onions and scatter over the parsley.

MY SECRET

You can make a batch of the onion base ahead of time if you want to make this recipe even quicker. Double or triple the quantity of onion then keep in a sealed container in the fridge for up to a week. Stir a spoonful into a stew or dollop on top of a soup.

Spiced MUSHROOM & *pine nut* omelette

Done well, omelettes can be deliciously satisfying and hugely indulgent. Think of the eggs as a blank canvas – they're simply a base to which you can add all kinds of ingredients. There are infinite varieties of omelettes in Lebanon which could easily constitute a book in itself. Here I've just gone for a version that uses my favourite tastes and textures, but you can experiment with your own.

SERVES 2

olive oil, for frying

2 large field mushrooms

2 spring onions, roughly chopped

15g pine nuts

½ tsp ground coriander

2 good pinches of dried chilli flakes

2 good pinches of chopped thyme

6 large eggs

small handful of chopped coriander

salt and ground black pepper

Heat a little oil in a large frying pan (with a lid) over a medium high heat. Cook the mushrooms, stalk-side up, for about 10 minutes, until they soften and colour. Lift them out of the pan and on to a plate, then add a little more oil to the pan and stir-fry the spring onions and pine nuts until softened and golden. Give the pan a good shake to flip the ingredients around, then return the mushrooms to the pan. Scatter over the ground coriander, chilli and thyme and give everything a good stir again with a wooden spoon so the veg are well flavoured with the spices.

Crack the eggs into a large bowl, throw in a good pinch of salt and whisk together. Pour into the pan, tucking the runny egg in and around the vegetables.

Use the wooden spoon to draw the setting egg away from the edge of the pan and allow the runny egg to fall into it and cook. Continue to do that until the omelette is looking thick and rippled all over. At this point, clamp a lid on top, turn the heat down low and allow the top to set. Scatter over the coriander then divide into two and serve.

Baked eggs *with* SUMAC, SPINACH *&* *spring* onions

Sumac, a crushed dried red berry, has a sour, astringent flavour a little like lemon. It's one of my favourite spices to serve with eggs and one that simply works. It's no coincidence that baked egg dishes crop up in many different cuisines; there's something brilliantly soothing about being served up an individual dish with an eggy jumble of ingredients.

SERVES 4

2 tsp olive oil

4 spring onions, roughly chopped

1 garlic clove, sliced

1 tsp ground coriander

pinch of dried chilli flakes

½ tsp sumac, plus extra to serve

200g baby spinach leaves

8 medium eggs

salt and ground black pepper

hot buttered toast, to serve

chilli sauce, to serve

Heat the oven to 200°C/180°C fan/gas 6.

Heat the oil in a large pan then add the spring onion, garlic, coriander, chilli, sumac and spinach. Season. Give everything a good stir and allow the spinach to wilt down in the heat of the pan. Turn the leaves over so the ones that haven't started to cook are underneath.

Roughly divide the mixture into four, then put each quarter into a shallow, ovenproof bowl or dish. Push it round the edge of the bowls so there's space in the middle for the eggs. Crack two eggs into each bowl.

Cover with foil and bake in the oven for 15–20 minutes or until set to how you like your eggs. Serve, sprinkled with sumac, with the hot toast and chilli sauce.

Comptoir *French toast*

1. Cut 4 thick slices of crusty bread, ideally from a loaf with a good flavour *2.* Very finely chop the stalks of a small handful of coriander or parsley (reserve the leaves) *3.* In a bowl, beat 4 large eggs with the chopped stalks, 2 tablespoons milk, 2 tablespoons crème fraîche and 1 very finely chopped green chilli. Season well with salt and pepper *4.* Pour the egg mixture into a dish large enough to lay the bread flat in *5.* Then, using your fingers or tongs, dip both sides of the bread into the egg mixture so it soaks in, flipping it a few times *6.* Put a frying pan over a low heat and add a good knob of butter and a drizzle of olive oil. Drain the bread slightly then carefully lower it into the pan with tongs or a fork. Fry the slices one at a time, sprinkling with sesame seeds, until golden on each side. Scatter over the coriander leaves and serve piping hot.

step by step

COMPTOIR rarebit

As you'll discover from various other recipes in this book – the Chilli Devilled Eggs (page 126) and Express Burger (page 186) to name just a couple – I love to mix up cuisines and cultures and take the best of each to create something new. The Welsh really hit upon a winner when they came up with the idea of rarebit. Melted cheese mixed with eggs, mustard, ale and various other punchy flavours, depending on how you like it, strikes me as genius. I'd happily leave it there. But a desire to experiment led me to create this Comptoir version using flavours that are more common to the Levant and thus more tempting to my palate. I've kept the iconic British cheese and the eggs, but I've spiced up the basic mixture with chilli, cumin and onion seeds to give it a stronger hit of piquancy. Served on thick slices of toast this is comfort food heaven, and the perfect melding of two great culinary cultures.

SERVES 4

100g each coarsely grated Cheddar and Feta, or all Cheddar if you prefer

4 spring onions, finely chopped

2 tbsp thick yoghurt

2 tsp onion seeds

2 tsp cumin seeds

2 tsp za'atar

large pinch of dried chilli flakes

2 medium eggs

4 large, thick slices of bread (about 2cm thick)

salt and ground black pepper

sesame seeds, to garnish

Heat the grill to high.

Put the cheese and spring onions in a bowl with the yoghurt, onion, cumin seeds, za'atar, chilli flakes and eggs. Season, then beat well to mix everything together.

Toast one side of the bread. Turn each piece over and spread about two tablespoons of the egg mixture over the top of each. Sprinkle with sesame seeds and grill until golden.

ZA'ATAR & chilli
devilled eggs

Classic devilled eggs are hard-boiled eggs, cut in half then filled with their mashed-up yolks mixed with a variety of other flavourings, such as mayonnaise and some kind of spice – mustard, chilli powder or cayenne pepper. I absolutely love them, but the ease with which they could be adapted to a Lebanese context meant that I couldn't help fiddling with the traditional recipe to use ingredients which are more common partners in my homeland, and more importantly, which I'm likely to have in my cupboard and fridge. I've swapped mayonnaise for the more tangy yoghurt, and have used za'atar in place of the hotter Western equivalents.

SERVES 4

6 large eggs

1 tbsp olive oil

1 tbsp thick yoghurt

pinch of dried chilli flakes

1 tsp za'atar, plus extra for sprinkling

4 coriander stalks, finely chopped

salt and ground black pepper

Put the kettle on. As soon as the kettle has boiled, pour into a medium pan and place over a medium heat. The water should be just bubbling but not too ferociously.

Lower the eggs into the water with a large metal spoon and simmer for 10 minutes. Lift out of the pan and place in a bowl of cold water. Allow the eggs to cool for a minute or two then peel.

Carefully slice each egg in half and tease the yolk out of its hole and into a bowl. Finely chop two of the white halves and add these to the bowl too. Break up the yolks with a fork until they are roughly crumbled then whisk in the olive oil, yoghurt and spices. Have a taste and adjust the seasoning to how you like it.

Arrange the egg white halves on a large platter. Spoon a little of the creamy yolk mixture into each one. Sprinkle the coriander stalks and a little extra za'atar over the top.

Tony's basturma & egg salad

Many Lebanese restaurants serve a bowl of chunky vegetables as an appetiser instead of a basket of bread, and it was from here that I drew my inspiration for this salad. The cured beef we use in Lebanon is called basturma and is essentially the Arabic version of pastrami cured in fenugreek, garlic and chilli. It's quite hard to find in the UK so I substitute it for the Italian bresaola which has a very similar flavour. Baked in the oven until crisp it gives a fabulous crunch to this salad.

SERVES 4

1 pitta bread, chopped into small squares

1 tbsp olive oil

1 garlic clove, crushed

12 thin slices of basturma or bresaola

150g green beans, halved

4 large eggs

2 Little Gem lettuces, leaves separated

bunch of radishes, quartered

150g cherry tomatoes, halved

¼ large cucumber, thinly sliced

for the dressing

3 tbsp extra virgin olive oil

juice of ½ lemon

handful of chopped dill

1 shallot, finely chopped

salt and ground black pepper

Heat the oven to 180°C/160°C fan/gas 4.

Put the pitta into a bowl with the oil and garlic. Toss everything together. Tip on to a baking sheet and bake until golden, turning halfway through. Place the basturma on a separate tray and bake 5–10 minutes until crisp.

Put the kettle on. Toss the green beans into a pan then cover with boiling water and turn the heat on to medium. Gently lower the eggs in too. Bring to the boil then simmer for 5–6 minutes until the beans are tender. The eggs will be done in this time, too. Drain well.

Put the lettuce leaves into a large bowl. Arrange the radish, cherry tomatoes and cucumber on top, followed by the green beans. Finally break up the basturma into bite-sized pieces and add these along with the pitta.

Peel the eggs and carefully slice in half. Lay on top of the salad. Whisk all the dressing ingredients together, spoon generously over the top and gently toss the salad, being careful not to break up the egg.

Grains & Pulses

BEIRUT BUTTERBEAN MASH 138

LENTIL & RAINBOW CHARD SOUP 140

BLACK-EYED BEANS WITH SPINACH & TOMATOES 142

FAST SPICED PILAF 146

SAFFRON, BUTTERNUT & RED PEPPER PILAF 148

HOT HALLOUMI PILAF WITH
BROAD BEANS, PEAS & HERBS 150

COMPTOIR LASAGNE 152

HARISSA, TOMATO AND SUJUK SAUCE
WITH VERMICELLI 156

BUTTERBEAN PILAF WITH SUN-DRIED TOMATOES 160

BULGAR PILAF 162

Grains & Pulses

For Levantine cooks, this chapter is one of the two most important in the book. Along with vegetables, grains and pulses form the foundations of Middle Eastern cooking and are generally the starting point for a dish or meal. Wheat and rice are the most common grains. Aside from the essential bread, wheat is found in the forms of bulgar, the cracked wheat used in core dishes such as tabbouleh and kibbeh, and couscous. Rice is the main ingredient in another staple – pilaf – and the five different recipes I've included here show how versatile it is but also the important place it holds in our cooking repertoire. For me, there are many wonderful things about a pilaf, among them the fact that it can be knocked together in under half an hour. Once everything's in the pan, it just sits and simmers until all the liquid has been absorbed, leaving you with light, fluffy spiced rice.

Beirut
butterbean mash

The title of this recipe is a bit of a liberty on my part because mash as we know it here in the UK – made with potatoes – wouldn't be served in Lebanon. Mashing up beans, however, is something we would do, so here I've combined the two concepts to create a hybrid dish. The mild, neutral flavour of butterbeans and potatoes is a perfect foil for the classic Lebanese seasonings of cumin and lemon, and the beans' creamy texture lifts the starchier, denser potatoes. You can choose how much to purée this depending on how smooth or coarse you like your mash.

SERVES 4

2 x 400g can butterbeans, drained and rinsed

250g potatoes, peeled and cut into cubes

400–500ml hot chicken or vegetable stock

2 garlic cloves, sliced

1 tsp ground cumin

2 tbsp tahini

2 tbsp extra virgin olive oil

½ lemon

1–2 tsp sumac (optional)

salt and ground black pepper

Tip the butterbeans into a pan with the potato, then pour in the hot stock. Add the garlic and cumin to the pan and season well. Put a lid on the pan and bring to the boil, then turn the heat down low and simmer for 5–10 minutes or until the potato and garlic feel tender when pressed with a knife.

Drain all the stock into a jug, then return about 100ml to the pan. Using a potato masher or a stick blender, purée until smooth. Beat in more of the stock until the mash is as firm or as soft as you like it. Any remaining stock can be kept in the fridge and re-used in a soup.

Beat in the tahini, half the olive oil, a good squeeze of lemon juice and the sumac to taste, if using. Check the seasoning – it may need a little more salt at this stage.

Spoon into a serving bowl and drizzle with the remaining oil and a little extra salt and pepper.

MY SECRET
To make this into a smooth hot dip, simmer the beans with 200ml stock then purée as above. Taste and season, stirring in lemon juice and extra virgin olive oil for extra flavour.

Lentil & rainbow chard soup

Grown all along the Mediterranean coastline, chard, along with spinach and cabbage, is one of the most popular green vegetables used in Middle Eastern cooking, now hailed around the world for its highly nutritious properties. Bunches of what is sold as 'rainbow chard' are actually just a mixture of a few varieties – Swiss, golden and red – each with a slightly different flavour: earthy, nutty and sweet. If you can't find rainbow chard, just go for Swiss chard, which is more widely available, or use spinach leaves in place of the chard leaves (ideally the hardy leaves with the thick stalks).

SERVES 4

1 onion, chopped

1 tbsp olive oil

100g rainbow chard

2 garlic cloves, chopped

1 tsp ground cumin

225g green lentils

1.2 litres hot chicken, lamb or vegetable stock

½ lemon

salt and ground black pepper

Put the onion in a pan with the olive oil. Cook over a medium heat for 10 minutes until the onion starts to turn golden at the edges. Give the pan a shake every now and then to toss the onions around in the oil.

Finely chop the stems of the rainbow chard and stir into the glistening onions along with the garlic and cumin. Season well.

Add the lentils and stock, then put a lid on the pan and bring to a simmer. Turn the heat down low and cook for 30–35 minutes until the lentils are soft.

Chop the chard leaves, leaving any tiny ones whole to decorate the top of the soup, and stir into the soup along with a squeeze of lemon. Cook for 3–4 minutes until the leaves have softened then serve.

MY SECRET

If you prefer a smooth soup, cool the soup before adding the chopped chard leaves. Purée in a food processor or blender then pour the soup back into a pan, add the chard and heat through.

Black-eyed beans with spinach & tomatoes

Don't use the baby leaf spinach for this, which turns into a mush when overcooked. If you can, buy bunches of the hardy thick spinach with the roots still attached – the stalks give this recipe its texture. Serve these beans with towering piles of warm flatbreads to scoop and soak up every last mouthful.

SERVES 4

1 onion, sliced

1 tbsp olive oil

2 garlic cloves, sliced

2 tomatoes, chopped

1 tsp ground cumin

1 tsp coriander, plus a little extra

1 tsp paprika

1 tsp black onion seeds

200ml hot vegetable stock

1 x 400g can black-eyed beans, drained

200g spinach, roughly chopped

extra virgin olive oil, to finish

½ lemon

salt and ground black pepper

thick yoghurt, to serve

Put the onion into a pan with the oil and cook over a medium low heat for 5 minutes. Stir the garlic and tomatoes into the softened onions, along with the spices, and cook for a minute or two, until you can smell the garlicky aroma.

Pour the stock into the pan and season well. Bring to the boil. Add the beans to the tomato mixture then cook over a medium heat for 10 minutes so that the tomatoes cook down and the liquid reduces a little.

Stir in the spinach and allow to wilt. Drizzle over a little extra virgin olive oil and add a squeeze of lemon juice, then serve with a dollop of thick yoghurt and a dusting of ground coriander over the top.

Fast *spiced pilaf*

1. Peel and thinly slice 2 garlic cloves *2.* Put in a saucepan with 1 tablespoon olive oil, 1 cinnamon stick, 1 teaspoon cumin seeds and a good pinch of dried chilli flakes. Place over a medium heat and cook for 1–2 minutes or until you can smell the spices and they start to sizzle *3.* Stir in 225g basmati rice and seasoning and toss to coat the rice in the oil. Add 450ml boiling water, clamp a lid on the pan tightly and bring to the boil *4.* Turn the heat to the lowest setting and let the rice gently steam for 10–12 minutes or until all the liquid has been absorbed. Fluff up with a fork *5.* Transfer to a bowl and serve immediately *6.* To make 'jewelled rice', add 50g golden sultanas to the pan at the same time as adding the rice. The to serve stir the seeds from half a pomegranate and a handful of freshly chopped dill or parsley through the cooked rice.

Saffron, butternut & red pepper pilaf

Whether you know it as pilaf, pilau, pilav or plov, you will undoubtedly be familiar with this rice-based dish, which has infinite variations and is found across the Middle East and Asia. At its heart, a Middle Eastern pilaf is essentially a means of cooking rice so that each grain remains separate, and the most basic version is a lightly spiced, fluffy rice accompaniment. As you'll discover from several of the other recipes in this chapter, more elaborate interpretations are equally as common, as are variations on the grain used (see the bulgar version on page 162).

I've kept the spicing really subtle in this recipe to allow the sweetness of the squash and peppers to shine through, but if you want to add a kick of heat, stir in a good pinch of dried chilli flakes with the cumin and add an extra quarter-teaspoon of freshly ground black pepper too.

SERVES 4

2 tbsp olive oil

1 onion, chopped

1 celery stick, chopped

½ butternut squash (about 150g), peeled, deseeded and chopped

2 red peppers, deseeded and chopped

1 garlic clove, sliced

2 tsp cumin seeds

200g basmati rice

400ml hot vegetable or chicken stock

a large pinch of saffron threads (optional)

½ lemon

salt and ground black pepper

Put the oil in a medium pan then slide in the onion and celery. Cook over a medium heat for 5 minutes. Add the squash and peppers and continue to cook for a minute or so.

Add the garlic to the pan with the cumin, stir for 1–2 minutes until the garlic and spices start to release their musky aroma, then stir in the rice. Season well and pour in the hot stock and add the saffron, if using. Put a lid on tight and turn the heat down to the lowest setting and simmer for 10–12 minutes until all the liquid has been absorbed. You'll see that the rice will start to look fluffy on top.

Fluff up with a fork and squeeze enough lemon juice over to balance the flavours.

Hot halloumi pilaf with broad beans, peas & herbs

Although in the Middle East pilafs are generally considered an accompaniment to a meal and will be served alongside other meat or vegetable dishes to create a whole, I would happily have a bowl of this for my lunch or dinner and feel satisfied. The rice is the building block and the bulk; squeaky halloumi provides the protein and a fabulous textural contrast to the soft rice; and the broad beans and peas are the indispensable vegetable element. It's filling, comforting and balanced enough to sustain and nourish. All that and it's ready in under half an hour.

SERVES 4

4 spring onions, roughly chopped

1 tbsp olive oil

2 garlic cloves, sliced

2 tsp nigella seeds

100g podded fresh peas (see tip) or frozen peas

100g podded broad beans (see tip)

200g basmati rice

500ml hot vegetable or chicken stock

100g halloumi, chopped into small cubes

small handful of freshly chopped mint, dill and parsley

salt and ground black pepper

Fry the spring onions in the oil for a few minutes over a medium heat, until they've softened and are glistening and golden. Stir in the garlic and nigella seeds and cook just until the garlic softens and starts to turn golden.

Add the peas and broad beans, season well, then stir in the rice. Cook for a minute or two, then add the hot stock. Cover with a lid and bring to the boil. Turn the heat right down low and simmer for 10 minutes or until all the liquid has been absorbed.

Stir the halloumi into the rice while you're fluffing it up with a fork. Scatter over the herbs. Taste to check the seasoning and serve.

MY SECRET

If you're podding the peas and beans from fresh, you'll need a total weight of 300–350g before podding. If you're using frozen, there's no need to defrost them, just pour them into the pan.

Comptoir lasagne

Feta, tahini and yoghurt replace the Parmesan and béchamel sauce, while vegetables replace the mince in this Lebanese twist on a classic. Although you don't have to faff around making sauces I'll admit there is still a bit of work in this recipe – cooking lasagne generally needs time – but I've included it because it's really great cold so is an instant meal if it's already been cooked, and also because it can be prepared up to a day ahead then put in the oven when you're ready to eat.

SERVES 4–6

1 aubergine, cut into 2cm chunks

2 red peppers, cut into 2cm chunks

1 courgette, cut into 2cm chunks

2 tbsp olive oil

2 large tomatoes, cut into 2cm chunks

1 red onion, cut into 2cm chunks

2 tsp ground coriander

½ tsp dried chilli flakes

100g spinach

8–9 dried lasagne sheets

300g yoghurt

200g feta, crumbled

2 medium eggs

2-3 tbsp tahini

salt and ground black pepper

Heat the oven to 200°C/180°C fan/gas 6.

Put the aubergine, peppers and courgette into a large roasting tin and drizzle over the oil. Season, then toss everything together with a large metal spoon so the pieces are well coated in the oil. Roast in the oven for 30 minutes until golden.

Stir the tomatoes, onion and spices into the roasted veg. Put the tin back in the oven and roast again for another 10–15 minutes.

Steam the spinach leaves by putting them in a pan with a good splash of water and heat just to the point where they wilt, but not so they lose all their texture.

Blanch the lasagne sheets in boiling water for 8–10 minutes, until slightly softened, then lay two or three sheets on the bottom of an ovenproof dish, with around 1 litre capacity. Spread over half the roasted vegetables. Fill in any gaps with bits of spinach then dot over 50g of the yoghurt and 50g of the crumbled feta.

Do the same for the next layer, starting by covering the yoghurt and feta with three pasta sheets. Drizzle with any spinach water left over in the pan.

Finally cover with the remaining three pasta sheets. Whisk together the eggs, tahini and the rest of the yoghurt then season well. Spoon over the top layer of pasta and scatter the rest of the feta on top. Give it another season and bake in the oven for 30–40 minutes until the top is golden and the pasta feels soft when prodded with a knife.

Harissa, TOMATO & sujuk sauce *with* *vermicelli*

Now in the Lebanon there is a spiced mixed meat sausage called sujuk, made with pork usually but in texture a little like chorizo. If you cant find it then merguez also gives a great result. Here it adds a rich flavour to this simple Vermicelli mezze dish, especially good when given a chilli kick with harissa. Yes, to some this dish has an Italian feel, but then Italy owes much to the Arabic world so it's understandable that it might give that impression. It's also very good served as a simple sauce for cooked boiled potatoes.

SERVES 4

about 175g sujuk or mini merguez sausages

1 onion, chopped

2 tbsp olive oil

2 garlic cloves, chopped

1 tsp ground coriander

1 tsp ground cumin

½ tsp cayenne

½ tsp chilli flakes

1 x 400g can chopped tomatoes

400ml hot vegetable or chicken stock

2 tbsp pomegranate molasses

100g vermicelli

handful of chopped coriander

Fry the sliced sujuk or merguez sausage in a dry pan until they're cooked through then remove to a plate and leave until later. Return the pan to the hob, add the onion and olive oil then cook over a medium heat for about 10 minutes or until they start to soften.

Stir in the garlic and spices and cook for a minute or two until you can smell the aroma. Season well. Then stir in the pomegranate molasses and season to taste.

Pour the chopped tomatoes and stock into the pan, then put a lid on top and simmer over a medium heat for 10 minutes.

Stir in the vermicelli, then replace the lid and cook for about 2 minutes. The pasta will absorb lots of the liquid in the sauce and the dish will thicken. Stir in the coriander, season again then serve.

Cooked whole beans don't freeze that well as they tend to burst and turn mushy. But falafel mixture and simple bean purées do freeze well.

MASH LEFTOVER COOKED GRAINS and mix with egg, breadcrumbs and cooked meat or fish for a simple mezze fritter.

When boiling beans, flavour the cooking liquid: I like one crushed garlic clove, half a peeled onion, two bay leaves and one halved fresh chilli. After cooking and draining, discard the aromatics.

Need to go wheat-free? Lightly cooked quinoa can be used in place of bulgar wheat in salads and served as part of a mezze.

Beans can be stored in a container in a cool dry place for up to 3 years and still be good for cooking.

comptoir larder

grains & beans

Most grains or beans are interchangeable in recipes if you're careful about cooking times. If in doubt, cook the grain separately and stir through at the end.

WANT PILAF RICE TO HAVE A GOLDEN COLOUR? A Lebanese friend's trick is to cook a little sugar to a dark caramel then boil it with the rice.

Bulgar wheat, like couscous, is pre-cooked so only needs soaking until soft before using.

Leftover cooked grains can be used in salads or re-heated gently and served warm under cold creamy sauces like hummus.

FRESHER GRAINS COOK SLIGHTLY QUICKER THAN THOSE MORE THAN A YEAR OLD.

BUTTERBEAN pilaf
with *sun-dried* tomatoes

As you know, I'm a big fan of pilafs, but the great thing about this one in particular is that it is as good served cold as it is hot. Serve it warm for supper as a main dish with a refreshing tomato salad on the side or scale up the quantities to make more than you need, and hey presto – instant packed lunch or salady-style starter for the next day.

SERVES 4

4 spring onions, roughly chopped

1 garlic clove, roughly chopped

1 tbsp olive oil

1 teaspoon ground coriander

150g basmati rice

1 x 400g can butterbeans, drained and rinsed

250ml hot vegetable or chicken stock

50g sun-dried tomatoes preserved in oil, chopped

100g feta cheese, crumbled

small handful of chopped coriander

½ lemon

salt and ground black pepper

Put the spring onions and garlic in a pan with the olive oil. Cook over a medium heat for about 3 minutes until the spring onions have cooked down and look as if they've softened and are glistening and golden in the oil.

Stir in the ground coriander and rice, season well and cook for a minute. Add the butterbeans, then pour in the stock. Put a lid on and bring to the boil, then turn the heat down low and cook for 10 minutes or until all the liquid has been absorbed.

Fluff the rice up with a fork, then stir in the sun-dried tomatoes, feta and coriander. Squeeze over the juice from the lemon half just before serving.

Bulgar pilaf

Although the cooking principle is the same as in the traditional rice versions, using bulgar instead of rice in a pilaf completely changes the texture and essence of the dish – bulgar wheat has a lovely nutty texture. Here I've upped the crunch factor by adding pine nuts and pistachios to the mixture to create a deeply savoury side. It's the perfect complement to a soft, yielding main, such as the Seabass with Date Purée (page 82) or any grilled fish dish.

SERVES 4–6

2 red onions

1 celery stick

4 tbsp olive oil

2 garlic cloves, chopped

2 tsp cumin seeds

½ tsp ground cinnamon

½ tsp cayenne

1 tsp nigella seeds

1 x 400g can green or brown lentils, drained and rinsed

200g bulgar wheat

50g golden raisins

325ml hot vegetable or chicken stock

15g pine nuts

15g pistachio nuts (salted or unsalted according to preference)

small handful freshly chopped parsley

½ lemon

salt and ground black pepper

Chop one red onion and the celery and put them in a pan with 2 tablespoons of the olive oil. Cook over a medium heat for 3–5 minutes until the onion starts to turn golden.

Stir in the garlic and spices and cook for a minute or two until you can smell their aroma. Season well at this stage.

Add the lentils, bulgar wheat and raisins and stir to mix all the ingredients together. Pour the stock over the top then put a lid on the pan and bring to the boil. Turn the heat right down to the lowest setting and allow the bulgar to slowly steam in the liquid. If you want a nutty bite, do this for 10 minutes. For the bulgar to have a soft texture, cook for 14–15 minutes. Resist lifting the lid when the bulgar is cooking, or the precious steam will escape.

Meanwhile, finely slice the other red onion. Stir-fry in a frying pan with the remaining olive oil and the pine nuts and pistachios over a medium heat for 5–8 minutes until the onion caramelises and softens. The slivers will be golden and cooked down, and the nuts will have started to colour, too. Season well.

Fluff up the pilaf with a fork, stir in half the parsley and squeeze over the juice from the lemon half. Spoon into a bowl and top with the remaining parsley and the onion and nut mixture.

Wraps & Bread

FLATBREAD WITH CUMIN, ROOTS & HUMMUS 168

CHICKPEA & COURGETTE FRITTER WRAP 170

LEMON-MARINATED HALLOUMI IN PITTA 174

GRILLED CHICKEN & FRESH COLESLAW WRAP 178

SAUCY HARISSA PRAWN WRAP 182

SKEWERED LAMB & PEPPER WRAP 184

EXPRESS BURGER 186

Wraps & Bread

Bread is an essential part of Levantine cuisine and will be on the table at every mealtime in some form. Breads throughout the Levant are mainly flatbreads, though the types on offer can differ greatly from country to country. The type of bread you buy to make the recipes in this chapter is important. In the UK, 'wraps' are often made from the Mexican tortillas that are widely available but these are not what's called for here. Please do track down an authentic Middle Eastern flatbread to assemble my wraps. I was pleased to discover that most large supermarkets are now selling traditional flatbreads, where they're often labelled as 'khobez wraps' – khobez being the Arabic word for bread. Specialist shops are also popping up all over the place, and the internet is an excellent source for seeking out authentic produce. If you do catch the wrap bug you could try out different types of flatbread, or why not make your own.

Flatbread *with* cumin, roots & *hummus*

You can lift the flavour of simple root vegetables, like carrots and beetroot, with more than just butter and herbs. I find that when they're sautéed in good olive oil with spices like cumin, or cardamom, and salted to taste they become one of my favourite vegetable mezze dishes. Serve them hot in a wrap with a simple hummus, lots of salad, chilli sauce, garlic sauce (page 198) or thick yoghurt, and you have one stupendous vegetarian wrap, and one of the healthiest I know of. These root vegetables can be cooked ahead and reheated when you're ready to eat.

SERVES 4

3 carrots, peeled and chopped into chunks

3 beetroot, peeled and chopped into chunks

2 garlic cloves, sliced

1 tsp cumin seeds

1 tbsp olive oil

4 khobez wraps or other type of thin flatbread

small handful freshly chopped coriander

salt and ground black pepper

for the speedy hummus

1 x 400g can chickpeas, drained and rinsed

2–4 tbsp tahini, to taste

2 tbsp olive oil

juice of ½ lemon

salt, to taste

Put the carrot, beetroot and garlic in a large frying pan with the cumin and olive oil and place over a medium heat. Cook for about 10 minutes, tossing every now and then until the edges of the veg start to soften.

Add 3 tablespoons of water to the pan, season, and put a lid on top. Turn the heat down low and simmer for around 10 minutes or until the vegetables are nice and tender and all of the water has been absorbed.

Meanwhile, make the speedy hummus. Put the chickpeas into a food processor with the tahini, olive oil and lemon juice. Season well and whizz until smooth. Add a drizzle of water if the hummus is very thick.

Spread each flatbread with 1–2 tablespoons of hummus. Scatter the coriander on top of the cooked roots, then spoon on top of the hummus, top with salad and any sauces you like then wrap tightly and serve.

{ }

MY SECRET
When I want to give this heathy wrap a rich kick I simply add slices of halloumi shallow fried in olive oil.

Chickpea *and courgette fritter wrap*

step by step

1. Drain and rinse a 400g can chickpeas. Tip into a food processor *2.* Add a roughly chopped courgette (say 150g), 100g fresh breadcrumbs, 4 roughly chopped spring onions, 1 mashed, peeled garlic clove, 1 teaspoon ground coriander, 40g plain flour and the grated zest of a lemon. Season well, blitz until almost smooth then stir in another grated courgette *3.* Heat a film of olive oil in a frying pan. Either shape the fritter mixture into balls with a little extra flour, or drop spoonfuls of the mixture into the pan *4.* Cook both sides until golden then drain on kitchen paper *5.* Spread some hummus down the middle of 4 thin flatbreads. Add chopped tomatoes, the fritters and chopped coriander *6.* Squeeze over some lemon juice and add dollops of thick yoghurt then season and wrap tightly.

Lemon-*marinated* *halloumi* in pitta

At Comptoir we use halloumi with the same gusto as the Italians show to mozzarella, adding it generously when we use it. Now you can simply oil and sear it over a high heat to give its rubbery, squeaky exterior a crisp caramelised finish. It's fabulous cooked like that, but marinating it and serving it very simply gives it a new dimension and makes it even easier to get it on the table. Marination is very subtle and allows different flavours – in this case lemon and mint – to take more of a central role. If you don't have a griddle pan, use a heavy-based flat frying pan to sear the pitta bread instead.

SERVES 4

100g halloumi, sliced very thinly into small rectangles

¼ tsp dried mint

zest of ½ lemon

olive oil

4 wide flat pitta breads

salt and ground black pepper

Slide the halloumi slices into a shallow dish and scatter over the mint then the lemon zest. Season and drizzle over a little oil. Turn the pieces so they're coated in the herby oil mixture. You can do this up to a day ahead and store it in the fridge. Just remember to remove it from the fridge before serving – the cheese is best served as near to room temperature as possible, rather than fridge cold.

Get a griddle pan really hot by putting it over a medium heat for a couple of minutes.

Brush oil over one side of each pitta then place one, oil-side down, on to the griddle. Press down and cook for a couple of minutes until golden brown and toasted. Brush oil over the top side then flip over and do the same again. Repeat with the other pittas, then cut in half and serve with the marinated halloumi tucked inside.

Man'ousha is for the Lebanese what pizza is to the Italians. Cover your flatbread dough (page 13) with spiced minced lamb, za'atar and pine nuts then bake in an oven set at 220°C/200°C fan/gas 7 till crisp.

Cut spare pitta bread into cubes, bake in an oven set at 200°C/180°C fan/gas 6, until utterly crisp and dry (around 15–20 minutes) then spoon the hot chips into a clean jar and cover with olive oil. This ensures they stay crisp.

Have flatbread days, where you make, bake and freeze it. Clean up, forget about it then re-discover it. Just heat your beautiful bread through from frozen.

IF THE OVEN ISN'T ON *and you want to defrost flatbread just use a frying pan. Get it hot, then put the frozen bread inside; it will crisp as it thaws.*

GIVE THAT BURRITO A LEBANESE TWIST: *fill it with grilled lamb and peppers, hummus, labneh, garlic sauce and rice.*

comptoir larder

bread

A handful of breadcrumbs

added to mincemeat for kofta helps to keep the meat juicy during baking as it swells and holds the moisture and fat.

Make **CRISPY SPICED BREADCRUMBS,** with za'atar, chilli powder, olive oil and salt. Mix together then bake on a tray till crisp.

ANY LEFTOVER DOUGH from making bread makes excellent quick flatbreads. Just roll it as thin as you can and cook it each side in a frying pan set over a high heat.

OPEN UP A PITTA AND USE IT AS A PLATE; SERVE the food directly on to the bread so it takes less space and soaks up flavour.

FRESH BREADCRUMBS FREEZE WELL IN A SEALED CONTAINER, so crumb any leftover bread or flatbreads (easily done in a food processor) and store it this way.

Grilled chicken & fresh coleslaw WRAP

When you're making coleslaw, yoghurt and tahini or even just oil and lemon keeps the flavour of the vegetables delicate and bright, while mayonnaise can sometimes dull them. So here I've wrapped up a beautifully spiced grilled chicken and paired it with a very simple cabbage, carrot and courgette coleslaw flavoured with fresh dill, tahini and thick yoghurt. Big flavour with a little crunch, better than mayo to suit this spiced and freshly grilled chicken wrap.

SERVES 4

4 x 150g skinless, boneless chicken breasts

1 onion, quartered

2 tsp each ground cinnamon, paprika, coriander, and dried oregano

1 tsp ground allspice

olive oil, for brushing

salt and ground black pepper

4 khobez wraps or other type of thin flatbread

for the fresh coleslaw

¼ white cabbage and ¼ red cabbage, finely shredded

1 carrot, coarsely grated

1 courgette, coarsely grated

handful of chopped dill

2 tbsp each olive oil, tahini and thick yoghurt

juice of ½ lemon

salt, to taste

Cut the chicken into bite-size chunks. Put the onion and chicken into a shallow dish and scatter over the spices and oregano. Toss the chicken in the mixture and season well.

Heat the grill to high. Thread the chicken on to skewers, then brush with a little oil. Grill until golden on each side, turning them every 5 minutes.

Meanwhile, prepare the coleslaw. Put the vegetables and dill in a bowl, then stir in the olive oil, yoghurt, tahini and the lemon juice, then season with salt to taste.

Spread a large spoonful of coleslaw on top of each wrap, add the chicken skewer, wrap up tightly and serve.

MY SECRET

Onion is delicious with grilled chicken so, if you like, add some sliced red onion, or chargrilled sliced white onions into this wrap. If you salt them lightly while they're grilling they'll soften quicker.

Saucy harissa prawn WRAP

As a child growing up in Algeria, harissa (chilli paste) was as familiar to me as tomato ketchup for most kids today. So as an adult I like to sneak it onto the table even for Lebanese cooking, and for this simple prawn mezze I find its fiery edge essential. You'll be left with a generous quantity of the delectable harissa tomato sauce, and it's quite a challenge to eat this wrap standing up without 'saucing' yourself as well. My advice: get the plates out, get round a table, get the sauce-laden prawns in the middle and get your guests diving in to construct their own wraps. Napkins optional.

SERVES 4

1 tbsp olive oil

1 small onion, roughly chopped

2 garlic cloves, chopped

½ tsp ground turmeric

1 tsp ground cumin

2 tomatoes, roughly chopped

½ to 2 tsp harissa

400g peeled raw prawns

¼ iceberg lettuce, finely shredded

4 khobez wraps or other type of thin flatbread

juice of ½ lemon

handful of chopped parsley and coriander

salt and ground black pepper

sliced cucumber, chopped parsley, za'atar, and labneh or thick yogurt, to serve

Heat the oil in a frying pan over a low heat. Add the chopped onion to the pan then turn the heat up to medium and cook the onions, tossing every now and again for about 5–6 minutes until golden brown.

Stir in the garlic, turmeric and cumin and cook for a minute or two. Add the tomatoes, and just ½ tsp harissa to start with as you can add more later.

Add 3–4 tablespoons of water and turn the heat up so that the water is simmering. Keep it like this for a couple of minutes until the tomatoes cook down and start to look mushy and the sauce thickens. Then add extra harissa to taste, and season well with salt and pepper.

Add the prawns and toss in the heat of the pan every now and then until they turn from grey to pink.

Scatter the lettuce over the wraps. Drizzle the lemon juice over the prawns then toss over the herbs. Divide the prawns among the wraps then top each with sliced cucumber, chopped parsley, za'atar, and labneh or thick yogurt to serve.

Skewered lamb & pepper wrap

Grilling skewers of meat over hot coals is the most traditional way to cook and serve meat in the Levant. The meat takes centre stage but it will be bolstered by a healthy component of herbs and salad to add freshness and contrast. If you're lucky enough to be enjoying some sunshine where you are, this would be even better if you can add the charcoal flavour by cooking it on a barbecue, but grilling it under an oven grill works just as well on a rainy Tuesday night.

SERVES 4

4 x 175g lamb leg steaks, cut into bite-sized pieces

1 garlic clove, crushed

1 tsp paprika

2 tsp ground coriander

2 tsp ground cumin

1 red pepper, halved, deseeded and cut into chunks

olive oil, for brushing

¼ iceberg lettuce, finely sliced

¼ cucumber, finely sliced

2 tomatoes, finely sliced

4 khobez wraps or other type of thin flatbread

½ lemon

2 tbsp yoghurt

salt and ground black pepper

Heat the grill to high.

Put the lamb into a shallow container. Add the garlic and spices, season well and stir everything together so that the lamb is evenly coated in the marinade.

Thread the red pepper and lamb pieces evenly on to four skewers. Brush with oil and grill for 8–10 minutes on each side, turning once, until the lamb is browned on the outside but still pink in the middle.

Put a handful of each of the lettuce, cucumber and tomatoes in the middle of each flatbread. Squeeze over a little lemon juice and season with salt. Top each flatbread with a skewer, season with more lemon juice and put a spoonful of yoghurt on top.

Express *Burger*

So many civilisations and historical interventions have left their mark on Lebanese culture, which in turn has led to a very diverse cuisine. At Comptoir, I try to reflect this past and like to offer our customers the essence of Lebanese cuisine but I'm also aware that as restaurants in the heart of London we need to cater to Western palates. Creating a Comptoir-esque version of the burger allows me indulge this clash of cultures. On the one hand the form and essence of a burger – minced meat shaped into patties – are almost a carbon copy of one of Lebanon's most traditional dishes, kofte, but on the other it's quite simply a universally loved dish, enjoyed around the world in countless forms. This version (which is astoundingly simple to whip up) flavours the meat with traditional Lebanese spices but serves it in a Western context – burger buns with salad. The Pomegranate Ketchup is a revelation and I'd really urge you to ditch the tomato stuff on this occasion – you won't regret it.

SERVES 4

for the burger

1 small onion, grated

500g lean minced beef

1 tsp dried thyme

2 tsp each of ground coriander, paprika, and sumac

zest of ½ lemon

vegetable oil, for frying

salt and ground black pepper

to serve

4 burger buns

¼ iceberg lettuce, shredded

Tahini Yoghurt Sauce (page 26)

1 beef tomato, sliced

½ red onion, finely sliced

Pomegranate Ketchup (page 23)

Put the grated onion into a bowl. Add the beef, thyme, spices and lemon zest and season well. Mix everything together well with your hands. Split the mixture into four even mounds then shape each into a burger.

Heat a little oil in a large frying pan over a medium low heat and fry the burgers for about 5–6 minutes. Turn over and continue to cook the other side until the burger is cooked through.

Split the burger buns and toast the cut-side of each lightly. Cover the base with lettuce then spoon a little tahini yoghurt sauce or mayonnaise over. Top with the burger, then the sliced tomato, red onion and pomegranate ketchup, then the top of the bun.

MY SECRET
Great with batata harra: potato cubes boiled till tender, drained, fried with diced red pepper in hot oil until crisp, tossed with chilli, fried sliced garlic, fresh coriander and lemon juice, then salt to taste. The business.

Express Essentials

COMPTOIR
LIBANAIS

Express Essentials

This chapter is a hotchpotch of recipes that I consider my vital tools for getting food on the table fast. They're the back-up team – ready to step in and rescue a solitary ingredient that's languishing in my fridge. Sauces are saviours for me – they can be whipped up in minutes and have an amazing ability to transform a single ingredient – say a lamb chop, a piece of grilled fish or a block of halloumi – into a dish that can tempt and tantalise. In the Middle East, people have a habit of dropping in for a visit without warning. And when that happens I want to be able to offer them a drink or a coffee and something to pick at while I get on with some cooking. So some home-made roasted nuts, olives that I've spiced up myself or some crunchy baked chickpeas are the perfect solution.

Butterbean *dip*

step by step

1. Make a dill pickle sauce (page 22), pour this into a bowl and set aside *2.* Tip a 400g tin of rinsed and drained butterbeans into a food processor with 1 teaspoon ground coriander and 1 teaspoon sumac. Peel and crush 1 fat clove of garlic with the back of a knife, mash it to a coarse paste and pop that in to the food processor bowl with the other ingredients *3.* Add about 3 tablespoons tahini and 3 tablespoons extra virgin olive oil *4.* Squeeze in the juice of a lemon with ½ teaspoon salt and lots of freshly ground black pepper *5.* Whizz every together until almost smooth, adding a squeeze more lemon or a couple of tablespoons of water if the mixture is very thick. Taste the dip and season with salt and pepper to taste *6.* Spoon into a bowl, sprinkle on more sumac and swirl on the dill pickle sauce to serve.

Tahini
tomato SAUCE

Although sesame seeds have quite a distinct flavour, once they're mixed with oil and turned into a creamy tahini, this strength is mellowed. Tahini is a pillar of Middle Eastern cooking and is used in so many different ways, for its flavour, texture or density. Here it transforms a simple tomato base into a luxuriously unctuous sauce – delicious spooned over a piece of grilled fish or chicken and a must for the Comptoir Mixed Grill (page 104).

SERVES 4–6

1 tbsp olive oil

1 small onion, roughly chopped

1 tsp coriander seeds

1 garlic clove

1 red chilli, deseeded and chopped

1 x 200g can plum tomatoes

100ml hot vegetable stock

50g light tahini

lemon juice

salt and ground black pepper

Pour the oil into a pan. Stir in the chopped onion and sauté over a medium–low heat for 10 minutes until golden tinges appear on the edges.

Add the coriander seeds, garlic and chilli and cook for a minute or two, again stirring around the base of the pan so that everything cooks evenly. Season well.

Pour in the tomatoes and stock and bring to the boil. Cover with a lid, turn the heat down low and simmer for 20–25 minutes.

Allow the mixture to cool, then whizz in a food processor until smooth. Whisk in the tahini sauce, add a squeeze of lemon juice to balance the acidity and taste to check the seasoning, adding more if you think it needs it.

Roasted garlic & YOGHURT sauce

Yoghurt sneaks its way into Middle Eastern food time and again, providing a lovely sourness and cooling foil to the hotter spices we cook with. Here it's part of the main act, mixed with sweet roasted garlic to create a deliciously moreish, catch-all sauce. It's an ace dip to accompany mezze but is also fabulous dolloped generously over spiced meat and fish dishes. It's particularly good with the One-Pot Fast Roast Chicken recipe (page 96). For big parties I make a huge batch at home, using about five heads of garlic baked in an ovenproof dish with foil on the top.

SERVES 4–6

1 garlic bulb

2 tbsp olive oil

125ml thick yoghurt

1 tsp tahini

lemon

salt

Heat the oven to 200°C/180°C fan/gas 6.

Put the garlic in the middle of a piece of tin foil, just big enough to cover the bulb. Pour 1 tablespoon of oil over the bulb, then pour in 50ml water.

Wrap the foil around the bulb tightly and put on a baking sheet, then bake in the oven for 25–30 minutes (depending on the size of the garlic bulb) or until the garlic is soft and tender. To check, unwrap and push the point of a sharp knife into one of the cloves.

Cut the end off the garlic bulb and peel away all the paper. Put all the exposed garlic into a mini food processor. Add the yoghurt and tahini and whizz until the mixture is smooth and has emulsified. Season with a good squeeze of lemon juice and a good pinch of salt.

MY SECRET

If you slice the top third off the garlic bulb and pick out the raw peeled tops, they make a great pickle. For every 100g of raw garlic, mix with 100ml water, 1 tablespoon of apple cider, 3 tablespoons of pomegranate molasses and 1 teaspoon of salt and simmer till slightly tender. It's best stored in the fridge and eaten cold.

CORIANDER *sauce*

This is a useful sauce to have up your sleeve as it's vibrant and light and pairs well with all kinds of dishes. I like to serve it over grilled halloumi to add a bit of zing to the cheese, but it's great simply stirred through lentils or as a fresh herby accompaniment to a stew.

SERVES 4–6

25g pistachios

1 tsp coriander seeds

60ml olive oil

1 garlic clove

40g coriander, roughly chopped

juice of ½ lemon

salt and ground black pepper

Put the pistachios, coriander seeds and 1 teaspoon of the olive oil in a frying pan and cook over a medium heat to toast the nuts – remove the pan from the heat as soon as they start to turn golden.

Crush the garlic clove on a board with a good pinch of salt.

Spoon the toasted pistachio mixture into a food processor then add the garlic and coriander. Pour in the remaining olive oil and the lemon juice. Whizz well until the mixture has become a paste. Add a tablespoon of hot water and whizz again to emulsify the sauce. Season with salt and pepper to taste, and thin the sauce with more olive oil if you want it more liquid.

Pour it into a sterilised jar and cover with a little oil. Seal, store in the fridge and eat within five days.

{ MY SECRET

it's really easy to double the quantities and make a big batch of this if you're serving a large number or want to have plenty of leftovers for the week. }

Pomegranate
HOT *sauce*

Be warned, this sauce is very, very hot – just how I like it! If you want a milder version go for large dried red chillies – you can often find them in Asian grocers or order them online. It's great with grilled meats or in place of some mustard on a burger. For something with the same pomegranate base, but a sauce you could serve to all palates, try my Pomegranate Ketchup (page 23).

SERVES 6–8

50g dried red chillies

1 tsp paprika

1 tsp cumin seeds

1 tsp coriander seeds

1 garlic clove, sliced

5 tbsp olive oil

2 tbsp pomegranate molasses

salt and ground black pepper

Put the chillies in a bowl and pour over enough boiling water to cover. Set aside to soak for 30 minutes. Drain well, discarding any stalks you see floating around and tip the soaked chillies into a mini blender.

Toast the paprika, cumin and coriander seeds in a dry frying pan for 10–20 seconds until fragrant. Add the garlic to the pan with 1 tablespoon of the olive oil. Cook for another 10 seconds.

Add the spiced oil to the blender with the remaining oil and the molasses. Whizz to chop finely then season to taste.

Quick pickled
CABBAGE

Being a nation of frugal cooks, Lebanon has a strong association with preserving, and pickling is one of the most ancient methods. Pickles are a constant at Lebanese meals as their acidity and freshness provides balance, and is good at cutting through some of the fattier cuts of meat. Traditional pickling will take weeks as the vegetables need time to ferment, allowing you to store them for several weeks. However, it's just as easy to achieve the same effect in flavour in a shorter time. This simplified version is left overnight and will keep in the fridge for up to five days.

SERVES 6–8

100ml red wine vinegar

1 tbsp salt

¼ small red cabbage

¼ small white cabbage

3 tbsp olive oil

2 tsp sesame seeds

small handful of chopped flat-leaf parsley

Pour the vinegar into a large bowl and stir in the salt. Put it to one side to let it dissolve while you prepare the cabbage.

Cut away all of the thick white core in the middle of the cabbage as this can be really tough to eat. Finely slice piece and put in a large bowl. Pour over the vinegar solution and stir really well.

Cover the bowl and put it in the fridge overnight or for at least eight hours, stirring every couple of hours.

Drain the vinegar solution from the cabbage, then stir in the olive oil. Toast the sesame seeds in a frying pan – there's no need to use any oil – until they're just golden. Stir into the cabbage with the parsley and serve.

FRY THAT PICKLE: sliced dill pickles, turnips or green chillies can be DIPPED IN BATTER (such as the one on page 100) and either shallow- or deep-fried then served with salt flakes and chopped herbs.

IF YOU'RE PICKLE SHY AND WANT TO EXPERIMENT, TRY SLICING THE PICKLES AND ADDING A FEW TO A WRAP OR SERVING WITH GRILLED MEAT.

PICKLE AND SAUCE COMBO: mix finely chopped pickles through any of the sauces and use as a dressing for boiled potatoes.

GRATE RAW VEGETABLES, LIKE THE FRENCH DO with their carottes râpées, then mix with any of the sauces in this chapter and season to taste.

MIX FINELY CHOPPED PICKLES through mayonnaise or labneh flavoured with herbs or harissa to use as a sauce with seafood.

comptoir larder

pickles & sauces

Want emergency pickles? Very finely slice raw peeled turnip and beetroot then marinate in apple vinegar, seasoned with salt and garlic, for 2–3 hours.

SUPERCHARGE THAI ROAST CHICKEN. Spoon any of the sauces under the chicken skin, then cook it as usual. Big flavour for little effort!

Sauces are generally brilliant doubling as MARINADES FOR MEAT or fish.

Get in the habit of putting pickles on the table at every meal. Pickles make life better.

Toothpick skewers of mixed pickles – sliced chilli, turnip and olive – are my favourite bar snack.

Spiced olives, *three ways*

Olives are an important part of Lebanese agriculture so it's natural that they should appear in such abundance on our tables. A mezze spread will undoubtedly include a bowl of juicy olives but you're just as likely to see them at breakfast time. While your palate may not be quite accustomed to their sharp savoury hit in the morning, the options below make a great accompaniment to drinks or as part of a mezze.

SERVES 6–8

200g olives in brine, drained

2 tbsp extra virgin olive oil

Red pepper and rosemary

½ marinated red pepper, chopped

1 garlic clove, crushed

1 rosemary sprig, roughly chopped

or coriander and garlic

1 garlic clove, sliced

10 stems coriander, finely chopped

or chilli and thyme

½ tsp dried chilli flakes

6 thyme sprigs, roughly chopped

¼ lemon, roughly chopped

Whichever flavour you're making, put the olives in a bowl with the oil and add the rest of the ingredients. Stir everything together well, cover and chill for a day to marinate before serving.

MY SECRET

If I ruled the world there would be olives on every table and at every meal, even at breakfast. So a recipe like this can be tweaked to suit your tastebuds, ensuring you always have olives on hand to help make this dream come true. Bring on the olives!

Chilli & Honey Roasted *almonds*

As a way of greeting guests and serving something inviting alongside a first drink, a bowl of spicy nuts really does it for me. Roasting your own by mixing them with spices, and here, a touch of honey, is not only going to impress your guests, it gives you something that really is a million miles from a packet of ready-roasted peanuts. These salty, sweet and spicy almonds can be rustled up in 15 minutes then left to cool.

SERVES 6–8

200g blanched almonds

seeds from 5 cardamom pods, ground

2 tsp ground cinnamon

1 tsp ground cloves

good pinch or two of chilli powder

4 tbsp honey

2 tbsp olive oil

salt

Heat the oven to 200°C/180°C fan/gas 6.

Tip the almonds into a large roasting tin. Give the tin a good shake to spread them out so they sit in an even layer, then scatter the spices over the nuts.

Whisk together the honey and olive oil and stir into the nuts, ensuring that they're all coated in a sticky layer. Roast in the oven for 10 minutes, stirring halfway through, until golden and toasted. Drain off the oil then scoop into a bowl, sprinkle with salt and allow to cool completely as they're a bit sticky at this stage, then serve.

Spicy roasted *chickpeas*

It's lucky pulses are good for you, because I find these crunchy spiced chickpeas seriously addictive. Sure, they take a bit longer to prepare than if you were to hand round a bowl of crisps but they're so much more satisfying. I serve them with drinks but also toss them into salads or sprinkle them over hummus and other dips for a crispy hit of spice.

SERVES 4

1 x 400g can chickpeas, drained and rinsed

1 tsp ground cumin

1 tsp ground coriander

½ tsp garlic salt

½ tsp paprika

½ tsp dried thyme

½ tsp sumac

½ tsp freshly ground black pepper

2 tsp olive oil

salt

Heat the oven to 200°C/180°C fan/gas 6.

Put the chickpeas into a roasting tin with the spices, olive oil and some salt. Toss everything together and roast for 30–40 minutes until golden and crunchy.

Toss them all again then try one to check the seasoning's right.

Sweets & Desserts

COMPTOIR LIBANAIS

Sweets & Desserts

Middle Easterners are renowned for their sweet tooth, but to my disappointment, dessert often gets overlooked. How often have you had guests round, only to realise too late that you've nothing to offer at the end of the meal, frantically opening your cupboards to search for a shop-bought cake, ice cream or some measly broken up squares of chocolate? Serving a home-made dessert or sweet at the end of a meal doesn't have to be time-consuming and is something that gives so much pleasure and feels special. Sure, I'm not going to be eating decadently sweet nut pastries (page 232) every day, but once in a while, they're a fabulous treat – so easy to whip up and an evocative taste of home. There are also plenty of healthy alternatives to a sugar-laden end to a meal. Granita (page 240), is wonderfully refreshing, while the Mango Parfait and Fresh Figs (page 244) would all count as one of your five-a-day!

Roast FIGS with *tahini* & carob sauce

Figs need to be served fat, juicy and very ripe, their dark purple skins almost bursting thanks to a healthy dose of sunshine. If you can't find figs that fit this description then I'd advise you not to attempt this recipe as it will simply disappoint. The sauce might sound like a strange medley of flavours, but trust me it works. It's brilliantly balanced – not too sweet, not too savoury – and is a lovely creamy counterfoil to the sweet figs. You could also pair these figs with cheese – a labneh or a creamy goats' cheese would be ideal.

SERVES 4

8 ripe figs

2 tsp olive oil

2 tsp clear honey

salt

for the sauce

4 tbsp light tahini

2 tbsp clear honey

1 tsp ground cinnamon

1 tsp carob or cocoa powder

Heat the oven to 200°C/180°C fan/gas 6.

Slice each fig in half through the stalk and arrange cut-side up in an ovenproof dish, just large enough to squeeze them all in. Whisk together the oil, honey and a pinch of salt then pour over the figs and transfer the dish to the oven to roast for 20–30 minutes.

Meanwhile, make the sauce by stirring together the tahini, honey, cinnamon and carob in a bowl. Stir in 1–2 tablespoons of boiling water to make a smooth, runny consistency.

Divide the figs among serving plates, then drizzle over the sauce.

Chocolate
chickpea *pudding*

A simple rich dessert that I serve like a panna cotta, upturned on a small plate. Chickpeas add a rich flavour without the need for eggs and if you make it with almond milk you have an impressive dairy-free dessert. One of the flavours I miss from Lebanon is carob, and if you can find carob powder then do use it. Also, carob molasses spooned over the top before serving makes it even better. Make these a few days in advance for an even easier dessert.

MAKES 6

1 x 400g can chickpeas in water (without any added salt), drained and rinsed

400ml almond milk

1 tbsp cocoa or carob powder

50g clear honey

3 small sheets of gelatine (see tip)

100g whole almonds, toasted and roughly chopped

125g dark chocolate (50–70 per cent cocoa solids, dairy-free), broken up

carob molasses, to serve (optional)

Put the chickpeas and almond milk in a saucepan, bring to the boil, then turn the heat off. Stick the lid on and leave for 15 minutes to infuse. Put the mixture in a blender with the cocoa and blend until utterly smooth. Pour the mixture back into the same pan, mix in the honey and bring to the boil, stirring often, then remove the pan from the heat. Soak the gelatine sheets in cold water for 2–3 minutes until they barely soften, then lift out of the water and stir them into the chocolate mixture. Add the almonds and chocolate then stir very well until the chocolate has melted. Lightly oil six 200ml ramekins or timbales. Spoon or ladle the pudding mixture into the moulds and leave until cold then chill for 2–3 hours until firm.

To remove the puddings, dip the moulds in boiling water for a few seconds, then turn out on to plates. Drizzle with carob molasses before serving, if using.

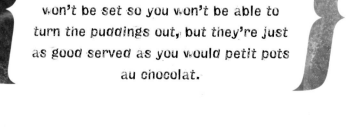

MY SECRET

If you want to make this without gelatine, just leave it out – the mixture won't be set so you won't be able to turn the puddings out, but they're just as good served as you would petit pots au chocolat.

Pistachio & ALMOND CAKE

I've given a very rough serving quantity for this nutty, dense and rich cake. You could serve it in thin slivers as a perfect sweet hit to accompany a bitter coffee, in which case it will stretch to about 20, but you could also serve it as a dessert, where you can be more generous with your portion sizes and it will serve about 10. For dessert I'd accompany it with a large bowl of thick yoghurt or crème fraîche to cut through the richness. The cake can sink in the middle so if you want to avoid this, bake it in a ring tin, buttered and dusted with flour inside, or as individual cakes in cupcake cases in a deep muffin tray.

SERVES 10–20

25g pistachio nuts, plus a few extra chopped nuts to decorate

185g unsalted butter, softened

185g golden caster sugar

3 medium eggs

100g ground almonds

85g semolina

2 tsp baking powder

juice of ½ lemon

1 tbsp clear honey

Grease a 20cm loose-bottomed cake tin then line it with non-stick baking paper. Heat the oven to 180°C/160°C fan/gas 4.

Whizz the pistachios in a blender until finely ground, pulsing the mixture so the nuts don't become greasy.

Put the butter into a large bowl. Add the sugar, eggs, ground almonds, semolina, baking powder and ground pistachios. Whisk well using an electric hand whisk until everything is mixed together. Spoon into the tin and bake for 40 minutes, until golden.

Stir together the lemon juice and honey. Take the cake out of the oven and pour the honey mixture all over the top. Leave to cool before scattering over chopped pistachios and serving.

MY SECRET

I like to serve this with a saffron syrup, made by soaking a pinch of saffron threads in 75ml of boiling water until the liquid is a rich golden colour. Add 100g caster sugar, heat until the sugar dissolves then spoon over the warm cake and serve with chopped pistachios on top.

Rose *tea-infused* dried fruit with TOASTED PISTACHIOS

A simple, spiced fruit dessert that can be prepared well in advance and whipped out as the occasion demands. It can sit in the fridge for up to five days where the flavours will continue to infuse and deepen, and it's also great for breakfast – on its own or topped with a generous dollop of thick yoghurt. You can add rosewater at the end if you prefer a more intense rose flavour, or replace it with orange blossom water if you prefer.

SERVES 4–6

8 cardamom pods

2 rose-scented black teabags or Earl Grey teabags

50g golden caster sugar

1 cinnamon stick

4 cloves

500g dried fruit, such as prunes, apples, plums, apricots

½ tsp rosewater, optional

25g pistachio nuts, roughly chopped

Gently crush the cardamom pods with the back of a knife to split open the pod. Drop the aromatic seeds inside into a medium pan.

Add the teabags, sugar, cinnamon and cloves and pour in 400ml cold water. Bring to the boil and simmer for 5 minutes. If you have time at this stage, whip out the teabags then allow the brew to cool completely – this gives it a fuller spiced flavour.

Put the dried fruit into a bowl and strain over the fragrant tea. Leave to soak for at least 8 hours or overnight, then check the flavour. You can add a little (say ½ tsp) rosewater if you want the floral aroma to be more intense.

Toast the pistachios in a dry pan until golden. Spoon the fruit salad into serving bowls then sprinkle over the nuts to serve.

ROSE syrup
pancakes

Rose is a widely used flavouring in the Middle East, used as petals, rose-water and essence Rose water is more diluted and has a milder flavour than essence so I've gone for the latter here, as the rose really is the hero of the dish, lending a fragrant Eastern twist to the familiar Western breakfast or dessert.

SERVES 6
(MAKES 24 PANCAKES)

for the syrup

100g golden caster sugar

1 tbsp rose essence

1 lemon

for the pancake

150g plain flour

1 tsp baking powder

1 tbsp golden caster sugar

1 medium egg

150–200ml milk

unsalted butter

vegetable oil

Put the sugar and rose essence into a pan. Pare a long strip of lemon peel then give it a twist to extract the oil. Drop the strip into the pan. Add a squeeze of lemon juice. Pour 100ml water into the pan then bring to the boil. Simmer for about 10 minutes until syrupy. Discard the lemon twist and leave to cool.

Sift the flour and baking powder into a bowl, stir in the sugar, make a well in the middle and crack in the egg. Start to stir the egg into the mixture, slowly adding the milk. Continue until all the milk is incorporated into a smooth batter. Set the mixture aside for 20 minutes.

Put a little butter and oil into a frying pan. Heat gently until the butter has melted and stops foaming, then tilt the pan to swirl it around the base. With a large tablespoon, place three rounds of batter into the pan. Allow them to cook over a medium heat for around 30–40 seconds then flip over and cook the other side. Continue to make pancakes until the batter is used up, adding butter and oil as needed. Keep the pancakes warm in a parcel of foil while you finish cooking. Drizzle with the syrup and serve.

MY SECRET

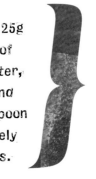

Serve with a Lebanese-inspired cream: beat 125g ricotta with 50ml double cream, 1 teaspoon of orange blossom water, 1 teaspoon of rose water, 1 tablespoon of lemon juice, a pinch of ground cinnamon and 1 tablespoon of caster sugar. Spoon this over the pancakes and sprinkle with finely chopped pistachios and candied rose petals.

Baklava-style NUT PASTRIES

The Turks, Greeks and Lebanese will all try to claim it as their own, but the word 'baklava' is in fact a generic term, used across parts of the Mediterranean and Middle East to describe sweet pastries made from filo pastry, filled with nuts and soaked in a sugar syrup (often flavoured) or honey. There are countless variations and interpretations but the main aim with my recipe was to keep it easy to prepare and, of course, to use some of my own favourite flavours. There's no elaborate layering of the filo here – a rich and fruity nut, pomegranate and date filling is simply wrapped up in a thin layer of the pastry.

MAKES 12

6 cardamom pods

50g golden caster sugar

100g mixed nuts, such as almonds, pine nuts, pistachios and walnuts

12 dates, pitted

1 tbsp pomegranate molasses

100g unsalted butter

6 sheets filo pastry

icing sugar, to dust

salt

Heat the oven to 200°C/180°C fan/gas 6. Line a large baking sheet with non-stick baking paper.

Break the cardamom pods open and drop the aromatic seeds into a food processor with the sugar, nuts and dates. Season with a pinch of salt. Pulse the mixture until the nuts are finely chopped and the dates help to bind everything together into a paste. Spoon into a bowl and stir in the pomegranate molasses.

Melt the butter over a low heat. Put one sheet of filo pastry on a large board so the longest side is facing towards you then cut in half down the middle. Brush one side all over with butter then place the other half on top. Cut it down the middle again to make two thinner rectangles.

Put about half a tablespoon of the nut mixture on the bottom of each strip then brush the exposed pastry with the butter. Roll up, folding in the edges to make a parcel. This may sound like a bit of a fiddle, but they're easy once you've done one and very quick to prepare the batch.

Brush liberally again with butter and arrange spaced apart on the baking paper. Do the same with the other five sheets of filo, the nut mixture and the butter until you've made 12 parcels.

Bake in the oven for 15–20 minutes until golden. Dust liberally with icing sugar and serve warm.

A shot glass of arak and ice

is the perfect afternoon relaxer. Then sleep before dinner.

GO A BIT 1970s: fresh strawberries dipped in melted dark chocolate sit well beside fresh mint tea.

To intensify *the colour of a honey syrup* make a dark sugar caramel first and mix the two together.

I truly believe fresh fruit after dinner helps you digest food. Slices of watermelon are my favourite.

Mix **leftover jam** with rosewater and warm gently for a *Turkish-delight* style sauce for ice cream.

comptoir larder

sweets

For a really tasty breakfast, mix thick yoghurt with mashed fruit and sugar, to taste, the night before – the fruit flavour infuses the yoghurt.

Roast nuts then layer them in a sterilised jar with good honey. THEY MAKE AN EXCELLENT QUICK DESSERT SPOONED OVER LABNEH AND WILL KEEP FOR UP TO 3 WEEKS IN THE FRIDGE.

Flavour honey with chopped herbs and za'atar then use it as a sweet basting for grilled meats.

Fruits such as **melon, mango, pineapple** can be peeled, covered and chilled before dinner then sliced just before serving. It saves you time but keeps the fruit fresh.

Mix a little arak with sweet lime cordial and freeze – PERFECT SPOONED OVER FRUIT SALAD.

CINNAMON *custard* WITH grilled PLUMS

Loved and hated in equal measure, to some custard is the scourge of school dinners – watery, thin and insipid – while to others it's the ultimate comfort food. I can say that I'm firmly in the latter camp. To me custard is thick, eggy, rich and soothing and I could happily hoover up a bowl of it on its own, but I also like it paired with fruit – banana custard being a favourite. Here, simply adding a touch of ground cinnamon to a classic recipe changes its whole character, instantly transporting me East, but purists can omit it and still enjoy a wonderful dessert.

SERVES 4

8 ripe plums, halved and stoned

15g unsalted butter

1 tbsp clear honey

zest and juice of 1 orange

for the custard

2 medium egg yolks

50g golden caster sugar

1 tsp clear honey

2 tbsp cornflour

1 tsp ground cinnamon, plus extra to sprinkle

300ml milk

Heat the grill to high.

Arrange the plums cut-side up in an ovenproof dish.

Beat together the butter, honey and orange zest then place a small piece on top of each plum half. Pour over the orange juice and grill for 15 minutes until golden.

In a medium bowl, beat together the egg yolks, sugar, honey, cornflour and cinnamon with 2 tablespoons of the milk.

Pour the rest of the milk into a pan and bring to the boil. Turn off the heat as soon as you see bubbles appearing at the edge and when the volume of milk starts to rise. Slowly pour the milk on to the egg yolk mixture, a splash at a time, stirring well with a wooden spoon. Pour the mixture back into the pan and heat gently until it thickens enough to coat the back of a wooden spoon, then turn off the heat.

To serve, layer the plums and custard in small glasses and sprinkle a pinch of cinnamon over each to finish.

Berry *yoghurt ice*

1. Split a vanilla pod down the middle, scrape its seeds then place them in a bowl with 600ml plain yoghurt *2.* Add about 100g caster sugar and 3 tablespoons honey, more to taste if you like it sweeter. Whisk until the vanilla seeds are evenly mixed though *3.* Freeze for 2–3 hours until ice crystals start to form. Scrape the frozen bits from the edge in and whisk lightly. Freeze again for 2–3 hours then scrape, whisk and freeze once more. If you have an ice-cream machine just pour into the machine and churn until smooth and almost frozen *4.* Fold 200–300g frozen berries into the cream *5.* Spoon the ice cream into a 900g loaf tin lined with cling film, pack down well then freeze until solid *6.* Best served slightly softened (poke a skewer in to check the softness), and serve scoops either in a bowl or a cone. Light, delicate and delicious.

Blood orange
mint *granita*

A searingly hot climate means that in the Levant we're constantly seeking ways to cool off. Ice cream parlours are a flourishing enterprise in Beirut and drinks served over crushed ice, usually flavoured with fresh fruit and syrups, are common across the Middle East. A granita is a wonderful combination of the two: lighter than an ice cream but denser than a drink. This fruity orange version is a wonderfully refreshing finish to a rich meal, or a cooling snack on a hot summer's day. Serving it in the hollowed out orange skins just ups the wow factor. Use any kind of orange if blood oranges aren't in season.

SERVES 4

6 blood oranges

100g golden caster sugar

large handful of fresh mint, including the stalks, plus a few extra leaves to serve

Put four of the oranges on a board and slice about a third to a half off the top of each. Take a small, sharp knife – it can be serrated if you have one – and carefully cut around inside the orange to separate the flesh from the pith.

Take out each piece and separate the segments from the flaps of skin and put in a food processor, discarding any seeds as you go. Squeeze the juice from the top parts of the oranges you've just cut off and put in the processor, too. Whizz to break down the pieces of orange. Put the hollowed-out orange skins in the freezer.

Squeeze the juice of the two remaining oranges and set aside.

Put the sugar in a pan with the mint and pour in 100ml water. Heat gently to dissolve the sugar in the water. Bring to the boil and simmer for 3–4 minutes or until you have a syrup.

Strain the syrup into a sealable container and stir in the reserved orange juice and the orange mixture from the food processor. Allow to cool, then freeze for 2 hours. The liquid will have partially set around the outside so fork through the mixture to mix the frozen with the liquid. Continue to do this about every hour, until the mixture is frozen but can still be forked through.

Fork through it once more and spoon into the frozen orange skins. Finely chop the extra mint leaves and sprinkle a couple on top of each orange then serve.

Mango parfait

At Comptoir, there aren't any rules around mealtimes. Dining with us means you can have anything you like at any time of the day, according to what you fancy. So while you'll find thick yoghurt accompanied by a selection of toppings among our breakfast offerings, turn to the dessert section of the menu and you'll find the same selection. Make up your own rules and serve this parfait whenever you want. Change the nuts, change the fruit and add whatever else you like – this recipe is a template not a mandate.

SERVES 4–6

30g almonds, roughly chopped

60g jumbo oats

2 tbsp pumpkin seeds

2 tbsp sesame seeds

4 tbsp clear honey

15g unsalted butter

1 tsp ground cinnamon

3 ripe mangoes, peeled and chopped

juice of 1 orange

200–300g thick yoghurt

salt

Put the almonds into a frying pan with the oats, seeds, honey and butter and cook over a medium heat until the butter has melted and the honey starts to run into the other ingredients. Stir everything together, toasting the nuts, seeds and oats in the heat of the pan. Sprinkle over the cinnamon and a pinch of salt and cook for a minute or two more until the mixture starts to set and clump together into little clusters.

Put about a third of the chopped mango into a mini food processor with the orange juice and purée until smooth.

Put a spoonful of the mango chunks into sundae glasses. Dollop the yoghurt on top, scatter over the oat and nut mixture then spoon over the puréed mango mixture.

Cocktails & Drinks

CARROT, CELERY AND GINGER
BREAKFAST JUICE 250

EXPRESS MANGO AND CARDAMOM JUICE 252

SPICED POMEGRANATE & YOGHURT SMOOTHIE 256

BASIL LEMONADE 260

BLOOD ORANGE & THYME SODA 260

CHAMPAGNE COCKTAIL WITH
FRESH POMEGRANATE 262

ARAK MOJITO 264

ROSATINI 266

POMEGRANATE G&T 266

FRESH MINT AND VODKA LIQUEUR 268

BANANA, TAHINI & CHOCOLATE SHAKE 270

SPICED LEBANESE HOT CHOCOLATE 272

Cocktails & Drinks

The climate across the Middle East is such that keeping cool is a constant priority and refreshment is key. One of the most popular iced drinks is jallab, made with a syrup of the same name. You pour the syrup into a glass, add water, plenty of ice and then spoon raisins and pine nuts over the top. This might sound a bit strange, so my two more local substitutes are home-made lemon and blood orange cordials, which you top up with sparkling water to make lemonade and orangeade. I love a good cocktail so I've also given you a few Lebanese twists on some classics, using flavours such as rose, mint and pomegranate. And if you're looking for something to serve alongside a pre-dinner tipple and haven't got your mezze in order, turn to the Express Essentials chapter for some salty, spicy solutions that can be ready in no time.

Carrot, CELERY & ginger breakfast juice

You'll need a juicer for this recipe and I know that's quite an investment but as those of you that have one will testify, once you've spent the money, you won't look back. Refreshing, energising and so unbelievably good for you, fresh juices really are all they're cracked up to be.

SERVES 1

3 carrots, roughly chopped

1 celery stick, roughly chopped

about 25g root ginger, roughly chopped

15g flat-leaf parsley

Chop the carrots, celery and ginger into chunks, then put through the juicer along with the parsley. Pour into a glass and enjoy.

MY SECRET

Of course vary the flavour as you prefer. Mix it with pomegranate or cranberry juice if you like more sweetness, or with grapefruit or a squeeze of lemon if you want it more sour. Drink it fresh as it discolours in the fridge, and if you prefer it cold then chill the vegetables first rather than dilute it with ice.

EXPRESS *mango* & cardamom *juice*

If ever there was a sweetheart of juices, one that seems to get everyone swooning, it's mango. In our Comptoir version we flavour it subtly with cardamom and lime juice. Get one that's still got some sharpness to it, not overly sweet, and you'll get the best flavour. Dilute the pulp as you need to as the thickness will vary depending on the ripeness of your mango. And if you're in the cocktail mood try adding a shot or two of arak and top up with soda water.

SERVES 2

2–3 cardamom pods

2 ripe mangoes, peeled, stoned and roughly chopped

juice of 1 lime

2 tsp clear honey

ice cubes, to serve

Break open the cardamom pods by resting a large knife on top of each and press down with the heel of your hand. Take out the little seeds, discard the pods and crush the seeds to a fine powder in a pestle and mortar.

Put the mango flesh in a food processor or blender along with the cardamom, lime juice and honey. Blend well until smooth and dilute with ice water if it's too thick.

Divide between two glasses, add a couple of ice cubes and serve.

MY SECRET
Add a large spoonful of natural yoghurt to the blender for a creamy mango smoothie.

Spiced pomegranate & YOGHURT smoothie

Here the gastronomic trinity of the Middle East – honey, pomegranate and yoghurt – are combined to make a delightfully simple yet tasty drink, perfect for breakfast or a snack. And if you like it even more fruit-packed just add berries.

SERVES 2

100ml thick plain yoghurt

150ml milk

2 tsp clear honey

the seeds from half a pomegranate, or 150g strawberries

2 tbsp pomegranate molasses

1 tsp ground allspice

pinch of salt

Put a couple of glasses into the freezer to chill quickly.

Pour the yoghurt and milk into a blender then add the honey, pomegranate seeds (or hulled strawberries), pomegranate molasses, allspice and salt. Whizz everything together then divide evenly between the two glasses, straining the seeds out as you pour.

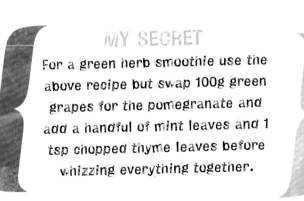

MY SECRET

For a green herb smoothie use the above recipe but swap 100g green grapes for the pomegranate and add a handful of mint leaves and 1 tsp chopped thyme leaves before whizzing everything together.

{ **AT COMPTOIR** we always have jugs of iced water with fresh mint on hand; I do the same at home.

For a really quick **REFRESHING LIME COOLER:** mix equal volumes of lime juice and caster sugar in a jug and leave in the fridge overnight. Dilute with soda water.

Add a few spoonfuls of arak to seafood soups — *the aniseed flavour is a great partner to shellfish.*

Wine isn't a huge drink in Lebanon, but when we do drink it we MAKE SURE IT'S SPECIAL and is the best we can afford.

USUALLY THE TIME WHEN I WANT FRESH JUICE *is not the time I want to do the juicing. C'est la vie, take me to the nearest Comptoir.*

comptoir larder

drinks

FREEZE JUICE in ice-cube trays and use to chill and flavour drinks.

Give iced coffee an Arabic touch with a little ground *cardamom* and *rosewater.*

TO SERVE ICED WATER with a citrus flavour, stick quartered limes and lemons on skewers in jugs — the sticks also make it easier to pour.

Blending fresh mint and thyme leaves with chilled apple juice and honey makes a great cooling summer drink.

FRESH MINT TEA is great kept in the fridge for a day or so; serve it iced with a squeeze of lime juice.

Basil *lemonade*

I've suggested serving this and the orangeade below with crushed ice. I think this makes these drinks even more refreshing and as you're already diluting the cordials with water, a little extra from the ice won't make much of a difference, but if you like a longer drink go for cubes.

MAKES 250ML CORDIAL

4 lemons, plus extra lemon slices to serve

100g golden caster sugar

20g basil, plus extra leaves to serve

crushed ice or ice cubes, to serve

sparkling water or soda water, to serve

Pare the rind from the lemons, making sure there's no bitter white pith. Place in a pan. Next, squeeze the juice of the lemons and pour into the pan along with the caster sugar. Roughly tear the basil sprigs across the middle and add to the pan then pour in 100ml cold water. Heat gently to dissolve the sugar.

Bring to the boil and simmer for 2–3 minutes until syrupy then remove from the heat and leave to cool. Once cool, strain into a sterilised jar.

To serve, put a handful of crushed ice into each glass, pour in 1–2 tablespoons of cordial, a couple of basil leaves and a slice of lemon and top up with sparkling water. The cordial will keep for 2–3 weeks in the fridge in a sealed sterilised container.

Blood orange **&** *thyme* soda

One of my favourite summer drinks, plus the cordial makes a great cocktail mixer.

MAKES 200ML CORDIAL

3 blood oranges

3 small sprigs thyme, or more to taste

100g golden caster sugar

crushed ice or ice cubes, to serve

sparkling water or soda water, to serve

Pare the rind from the oranges, cut into thin strips and put into a pan with the thyme.

Pour 100ml cold water into the pan, bring to the boil and simmer for 5 minutes to extract the flavour from the rind. Add the sugar and bubble until syrupy.

Remove from the heat, stir in the reserved orange juice and strain into a sterilised bottle or jar.

To serve, put a handful of crushed ice into each glass, pour in 3–4 tablespoons of cordial and top up with sparkling water. The cordial keeps up to a week covered in the fridge.

Champagne *cocktail* with FRESH *pomegranate*

A classic champagne cocktail is made by soaking a sugar cube in Angostura bitters, adding brandy to the bottom of the flute and topping it up with champagne. Here, I've softened the bitterness slightly, using tangy pomegranate to replace the Angostura. The fruit is made into a juice and mixed with the brandy and sugar before being poured into the glass, while a few extra seeds floating in the bubbles give it the visual impact of a dissolving sugar cube.

SERVES 6

1 x 750ml bottle of champagne, prosecco or cava

1 pomegranate

30g caster sugar

50ml brandy

Have your fizz chilled or, if it's at room temperature, put it in the freezer while you prepare the other ingredients.

Cut the pomegranate in half, then cut a small wedge from one piece and put to one side (these are the seeds to garnish the cocktail at the end).

Remove the seeds and place in a food processor, making sure there is no white pith attached to them. Whizz for a minute or two to extract the juice.

Strain the liquid into a small pan and add the sugar and brandy. Heat gently to dissolve the sugar then bring to the boil and simmer for 2 minutes. Leave to cool.

Remove the seeds from the small wedge of pomegranate and pop a few each into six champagne flutes. Divide the brandied pomegranate syrup equally among them then top up with the chilled fizz.

Arak mojito

step by step

1. For each drink: get a ripe juicy lime (check this by squeezing it, to see that it gives slightly) and cut it into quarters **2.** Put 2 teaspoons sugar and 20 mint leaves into a sturdy glass or shaker with the quartered lime **3.** Use the handle end of a wooden spoon to 'muddle' the mint, lime quarters and sugar together by pressing and pounding them down to extracting the oils, crush the fruit and mint, and dissolve the sugar **4.** Add a small handful of crushed ice or cubes to a serving glass **5.** Finally pour 15ml each of arak and rum over the crushed or cubed ice; add the lime, mint and sugar mixture and stir in more mint **6.** Top up with sparkling water or soda water, add a final sprig of mint to serve and enjoy immediately.

Rosatini

A classic martini given a Lebanese twist with rose water and a twist of orange. Make up the sugar syrup and keep it stored in the fridge so you can shake this up whenever the mood takes.

MAKES 10–20 DRINKS

for the sugar syrup

50g sugar

50ml cold water

1 tbsp rose water

for each rosatini

about 50–75ml gin

about 5ml vermouth

lots of ice

a twist of orange zest

Pour the sugar and water into a pan and heat gently to dissolve the sugar. As soon as all the crystals have disappeared and you don't see any more in the pan, bring to the boil. Simmer for 5 minutes then turn off the heat. Allow this syrup to cool then stir in the rose water. Pour into a sterilised bottle or jam jar and seal and keep in the fridge until you're ready to use.

Okay, it's cocktail time. A quick way to measure the gin is to three-quarters fill each martini glass and pour this into the shaker: that way you should have just the right amount of rosatini to fill each glass. Put 1 or 2 teaspoons of the sugar syrup into a cocktail shaker with the gin, vermouth and 6 or 8 cubes of ice. Secure the top and shake well – until the outside of the cocktail shaker is freezing cold. Strain the rosatini into the glass, toss in the orange zest and serve.

Pomegranate G&T

For the best flavour make this with fresh pomegranates. Cut the fruit in half, pull out the seeds with a spoon then bash them in a mortar and pestle (or with a few quick blasts in a food processor). If you use store-bought juice add a squeeze of lemon juice to give it more punch.

MAKES 1 TALL GLASS

60ml fresh pomegranate juice

2 tsp pomegranate molasses

a mint sprig

50ml gin

lots of ice

tonic

Pour the pomegranate juice, molasses and mint into a glass and stir well until the molasses is mixed through. Add the gin, fill the glass three quarters full of ice and top up with tonic to serve.

Fresh MINT & vodka *liqueur*

There's nothing more seductive to me than a huge bunch of fresh mint, and equally nothing more puzzling than how to use all of it. So that's where mint liqueur comes in, perfect to add to drinks and cocktails instead of sweetening with sugar. Now the colour turns to dark caramel, so it's best mixed with ingredients that suit that hue, like cola or a dark spirit like bourbon. Excellent too as the liqueur in a whisky sour, or mixed with arak and served over ice with a little mint.

MAKES ONE 350ML BOTTLE

350ml vodka

100g golden caster sugar

5 mint sprigs (about 12g)

1 tbsp coriander seeds

1 cinnamon stick

4 cloves

Pour the vodka into a 600ml sterilised jar or bottle. Add the sugar, mint sprigs, coriander, cinnamon and cloves then seal.

Leave in a cool, dark place for 5 days.

Strain into a clean sterilised bottle and serve over chilled ice.

MY SECRET

Wherever sugar syrup is called for in a recipe, I sometimes like to mix in a little mint liqueur at the end if it suits the other ingredients. So in poached pears, or on pancakes (page 230), or on soaked dried fruits (page 228) the syrup will add a subtle mint flavour.

Banana, *tahini* & CHOCOLATE shake

Thick, rich, creamy and cooling – with chocolate as well – for me this is the ultimate comfort milkshake. The tahini and brown sugar give it a flavour reminiscent of good halva, and the grated chocolate takes it perfectly over the top. Just what a great milkshake should be.

SERVES 2

1 banana, roughly chopped

50ml plain yoghurt

150ml milk

1 tbsp tahini

1 tbsp brown sugar

about 3 large scoops of vanilla ice cream

good pinch of ground cinnamon

15g dark chocolate (minimum 70 per cent cocoa solids)

Put the banana into a food processor with the yoghurt, milk, tahini, sugar, a large scoop of vanilla ice cream and cinnamon. Whizz to blend everything together.

Divide between two glasses, then add another scoop of ice cream to each one. Grate the dark chocolate over the top and serve.

{ **MY SECRET**
Add dark chocolate ice-cream in place of vanilla if you like, and if you want it to have some Brandy Alexander magic add a shot of espresso and a jigger of brandy. }

spiced Lebanese *hot* chocolate

A hot chocolate that's dark, rich and layered with spices. Adjust the spices to suit your taste – I like the kick the chilli gives – and add more honey if you like your drink sweeter.

SERVES 2

4 cardamom pods

1 tsp ground cinnamon

pinch of dried chilli flakes

pinch of salt

300ml milk

1 tsp clear honey

75g dark chocolate (minimum 70 per cent cocoa solids), finely chopped

Start by preparing the cardamom seeds. Break the pods open by resting a large knife on top of each and press down with the heel of your hand. Take out the little seeds, discard the pods and put them into a mortar. Add the cinnamon, chilli and salt and grind everything together using the pestle to make a fine powder. Pour the powder into a pan, then add the milk and honey.

Divide the dark chocolate between two mugs.

Bring the spiced milk to the boil then pour into the mugs. Stir well so that the melted chocolate is mixed into the spiced milk thoroughly and serve immediately.

{
MY SECRET
Is it ok to replace the dark chocolate with milk chocolate? Absolutely, but go for one that still has a rich flavour or mix it half and half with dark. }

DAN LEPARD *is an award-winning chef, author and food photographer, whose first book,* **Baking with Passion***, was published in 1999. He photographed Giorgio Locatelli's masterwork* **Made in Italy***, winner of the Glenfiddich and World Gourmand awards, and* **Hawksmoor at Home***, as well as his own books,* **The Handmade Loaf** *and* **Short & Sweet***, winner of the Andre Simon Award. Melbourne-born, Dan now spends most of his time in London, cooking, writing about and photographing food.*

IMOGEN FORTES *is a food and travel writer and editor. She works with chefs, food writers, restaurants and other brands, writing on their behalf to bring their ideas and expertise to life on the page. Co-author of the latest edition of* **The Rough Guide to Paris***, Imogen also pens food and travel features for a variety of publications. She collaborated with Tony, Dan and Emma to flavour the book with the Comptoir ethos and convey the ideas and inspiration behind the recipes.*

EMMA MARSDEN *is a food writer, stylist and author. Formerly the cookery editor of* **Good Housekeeping** *magazine, Emma creates recipes that are easy for anyone to do, with ingredients that are accessible to all. As well as her own book,* **Heart on a Plate***, Emma writes and styles for a number of major brands, including Fortnum & Mason and Sainsbury's. Emma worked closely with Tony and Dan to ensure that the recipes in this book reflect the relaxed, easy-going style of the cooking at Comptoir, as well as staying true to Middle Eastern flavours and culinary heritage, and the 'express' nature at the book's heart.*

NEAL TOWNSEND *is a graphic designer with over 30 years' experience in graphic design and print. He started out as a designer on the* **Melody Maker** *and then on to work on various BBC magazines –* **Gardeners' World** *and* **Vegetarian Good Food** *– before moving into book publishing where he has designed books for Random House, including the first Comptoir Libanais book and* **Semplice***.*

RANA SALAM *is one of the most celebrated graphic designers and artists from the Middle East. Rana has been running her own design studio for over a decade, producing distinctive work for her clients. Her unique knowledge of Arab culture and its popular art stems from years of travelling. Rana worked closely with Comptoir Libanais and Tony Kitous on the design of every element of the restaurant's look and feel, capturing the authentic atmosphere of the Middle East.*

acknowledgements

I would like to thank my friends and family for being there for me. My dearest mum Zohra who is the heart of my life – I love you. My business partner Chaker Hanna for being there for me, supporting me and allowing me to express myself in creating recipes and designing the interior of the restaurants. Dan Lepard for all his support and advice in co-writing this book with me and for the most beautiful pictures. My publisher Trevor Dolby for his encouragement and patience.

Our most amazing, hardworking team who strive to make all our guests' experience enjoyable and look after them. All our suppliers for supporting us and sourcing Middle Eastern ingredients and goodies.

Nicola Ibison, David Whitehouse, David Jones, Rana Salam, Richard Kleiner, Jan Glen, Sarah Brading, Kasia Dziadura, Neal Townsend, Nicola Evans, Rita Ferry and family; Moussa Bouguerra and family; Mohamed Lamari, Djamel Iratni, Paula Tahraoui and family; the team at Sirocco restaurant, Daphne Lerner, Adlene Guedioura, Hassen Guedioura, Kamel Abdellaoui, Haj Abdelhaq Moutacalli, Nasser Haouanouh, Helena Desave, Rebecca Bryan and Silvana Alves Ribeiro, Lorraine and Nigel McCormack.

My late Aunt Malika RIP, all my aunts and uncles, cousins, nephews and nieces, sisters-in-law and brothers-in-law. My sister Safia, my brothers Madjid, Salah, Ramedane, Mehdi and Mourad. My late father Haj Chabane Kitous RIP.

Finally, just before we were finishing this book my brother Salah had a very serious accident that left him fighting for his life. As we say back home, Hamdullah (thank God) he is now slowly recovering from his injuries. I would like to say a special thank you to the magnificent doctors, nurses and carers at the Richmond ICU in Beaumont Hospital in Dublin and the Tullamore General Hospital in Tullamore. They are incredible people, they do an amazing job – they save lives. I hope, Inshallah (God willing), by the time this book is published my brother Salah will be able to read this message. This book is for you.

Tony Kitous

INDEX

Published by Preface 2014

10 9 8 7 6 5 4 3 2 1

First published in Great Britain in 2014 by Preface Publishing
20 Vauxhall Bridge Road
London, SW1V 2SA

An imprint of The Random House Group Limited

www.randomhouse.co.uk

Addresses for companies within The Random House Group Limited
can be found at www.randomhouse.co.uk

The Random House Group Limited Reg. No. 954009

A CIP catalogue record for this book is available from the British Library

ISBN 978 1 848 09441 3

The Random House Group Limited supports the Forest Stewardship Council® (FSC®), the leading international
forest-certification organisation. Our books carrying the FSC label are printed on FSC®-certified paper. FSC is the
only forest-certification scheme supported by the leading environmental organisations, including Greenpeace. Our
paper procurement policy can be found at www.randomhouse.co.uk/environment

Designed by Neal Townsend
Cover concept by Rana Salam
Project editor: Nicola Evans
Sub-editor: David Whitehouse
Food stylist: Chris Taylor

Printed and bound in China by C&C Offset Printing Co. Ltd.